INDIAN AESTHETICS

K. S. RAMASWAMI SASTRI

GYAN

Published by

GYAN

Gyan Publishing House
5, Ansari Road
Daryaganj, New Delhi-110002
Phone: 011-47034999, 9811692060
E-mail: books@gyanbooks.com

Distribution Network
gyanbooks.com
India, USA, Canada, UK, Australia

ISBN: 978-93-6920-253-9 (PB)

First Published, 1928

2nd Impression 2025

Printed at: Gyan Press, Delhi.

INDIAN AESTHETICS
Author: K. S. RAMASWAMI SASTRI

INDIAN AESTHETICS

INDIAN ÆSTHETICS.

BY

K. S. RAMASWAMI SASTRI

Author of: *"Rabindranath Tagore Poet, Patriot, and Philosopher", "Hindu Culture", "An Epic of Indian Womanhood", "Rati Vijayam" "Bhagavad-Gita etc.*

SRIRANGAM:

SRI VANI VILAS PRESS.

1928.

PREFACE.

My aim in this work is to reveal how not only is outer India a home of beauty and romance but how inner India is even more truly such a home. Indian Art and Aesthetics have a history extending over thousands of years and it is well-nigh impossible to compress them into a tiny volume but I have assayed this difficult and ambitious task. The study of æsthetic values is not a mere bright and decorative but useless and purposeless purple patch on life. It has been well said that "æsthetic pleasure is our joy in the realisation of a universe, harmonious beyond the accidents of forms, united in a rhythm which has an echo in our own inner self." Mr. Bridges says in wise and lovely words: "Poetry being the most intimate expression of man's spirit, is necessary to education; since no man can be a worthy citizen of an earthly state, unless he be first a citizen of the heavenly". I claim that in the Indian renaissance of to-day, educational and industrial and political work is not more important than art and religion.

Indian Art is truly the mirror of India's soul, and is destined to be the real unifier of India and the true God-sent builder of the *Civitas Dei*..

TRICHINOPOLY
24—10—28.

K. S. Ramaswami Sastri.

CONTENTS.

INDIAN ÆSTHETICS.

CHAPTER I.

The Nature of Aesthetics in General.

AESTHETICS is the science of Beauty as expressed in Art. The sense of beauty has been, perhaps, along with the religious sense, the most distinctive charateristic of man. Standards and ideals of beauty have varied from age to age but the thrill of joy at the sight of beauty has been an ancient rapture. Nay, certain imperishable and eternal elements have been present in all conceptions of beauty whatever were the variations, due to time and place and race, which interwoven as woof with warp have brought about apparent divergences in the texture of beauty in the loom of eternity. Different thinkers have sought such elements of beauty in diverse ways and with diverse results.

I do not purpose to deal here with the theory of the beautiful as it has been expressed and discussed in various lands and in various times. My main purpose in this book is to deal with the theories of beauty and art as found in Indian Aesthetics. I shall however allow myself the freedom and the delight of dealing with the general principles of beauty and art and taste and style as I understand the same, before I proceed to deal with the main purpose of this work. I need hardly say that though my outlook will be largely coloured both by my Indian culture and by the modern age, I shall aim at a sincere and truthful and original presentation of such principles as I have found to underly all the universal conceptions of beauty and of art.

Man had art even before he had law or government. Even in prehistoric times he was fond of ornament and decoration. He sought to imitate Nature's forms in his handiwork. But it was only after he reached the agricultural stage that he had the necessary repose and leisure for observing and realising and expressing the beauty lying in abundance all around. Indeed the two pre-eminently human characteristics are love of knowledge and love of beauty. The instinct of animals leads them along the daily and unchanging round of search of food. But man's reason leads him to enjoy the knowledge of the Finite for its own sake and his intuition leads him to the knowledge of the Infinite. The emotional range of the animal is confined to mere reproduction and protection of offspring. Man's emotional range embraces not merely the family but includes country and humanity and nature. Nay, his love dares to realise in the heart and express by handiwork and song and speech the eternal and infinite beauty of things. His surplus energy of martial emotion is not content with the affirmation of his power but breaks forth into thrilling songs of patriotism. His surplus energy of erotic emotion is not content with marital union but breaks forth into rapturous songs of love. His surplus energy of altruistic emotion is not content with trying to do good to others but pulsates with a passion of extensive and intensive love which dreams utopias, utters in melodious words its conceptions of a higher world-order, and seeks to realise them in increasing perfection. His surplus energy of Godward emotion is not content with seeking to attain Him but fires his heart and his utterance with such fervour that his frame thrills under the spell of the inner bliss and his tongue thrills under the spell of the inner urge to expression. Just as his reason seeks to refer disconnected acts to the connecting focus of the central unity of divine intelligence, his love seeks to refer all radii of delight to the innermost centre of divine bliss.

Thus art is due to man's natural impulse towards beauty and love and truth and wisdom and goodness. To realise this we must realise the real man as different from the "unreal" man. I use the word "unreal" in the sense of "pathological" or "deprived of true self-expression". A healthy man is he who triumphantly affirms and realises his physical energy. An unhealthy man is he whose physical energy is over-borne by disease and is not capable of triumphant self-affirmation. Even so the real man is he whose real nature is in a state of triumphant self-realisation and self-affirmation. A jaundiced man will see everything yellow. He will not believe the affirmation of colours by the healthy eye. If he reverts to his state of health, only then he will have that privilege and delight. Even so, as long as our mind is overwhelmed by *Tamas* (inertia) or *Rajas* (attached and desireful and feverish activity), the reality of our nature is, as it were, enfolded by a sheath which denies outlet to our nature as all-perceiving and all-enjoying bliss, even as a dark cloud obstructs the free flow of sunlight and obscures the sun. But in *sattvic* moods of calm and repose and clear vision, there is a thinning of the veil. Just as a thin cloud nearing the moon becomes so full of the lunar light that it seems to become itself a second moon, even so the *sattvic* sheath becomes illumed by the joy of the soul. Every man has such moods of calm and clear vision now and then, especially during full-moon nights by the seashore or in the presence of youthful and innocent feminine loveliness or when beholding a graceful and blooming child or before perfect architecture or statuary or painting or when reading perfect poesy or hearing sweet melodies. He then realises how the *sattvic* state is natural to him and gives him the joy of self-expression while the *rajasic* and the *tamasic* states are unnatural and deny him the joy of self-expression. Art is thus the free play of the soul through the unobstructive and transparent medium of the *sattvic* state of the mind.

In this connection we must bear in mind the closely allied Indian philosophical concept of the Pancha kosas (or the five sheaths of the soul). Man has a physical sheath (the *sthula sarira*); he has a sheath of energy, a sheath of agitated mentality, and a sheath of calm and steadfast mentality (the *sukshma sarira*); and he has a sheath of bliss or Ananda (the *karana sarira*). The five sheaths are described also as the Annamaya kosa (the physical sheath or body), the Pranamayakosa (the sheath of energy), the *Manomayakosa* (the sheath of mind), the *Vijnamayakosa* the·(sheath of intellect) and the *Anandamaya kosa* (the sheath of bliss). The *sthula sarira* comprises the first sheath or *avarana* ; the *sukshma sarira* comprises the next three sheaths; and the *karana sarira* comprises the radiant and tenuous and translucent sheath which refracts the light of the world into the colours of beauty and refracts the white light of the soul into the prismatic colours of imaginative reason and emotion and intuition. It will be more appropriate to refer to the specialities of the Indian concepts on Aesthetics in a later chapter.

The idea of Beauty has been a very puzzling idea. The spirit of man has felt the sweetness and charm of Beauty in all ages and climes without having been ever able to account for such sensations of delight in the presence of Beauty or to define the origin and nature and essence and purpose and mission of Beauty. We speak of beautiful scenery, beautiful eyes, beautiful deeds, beautiful words and beautiful thoughts. Does beauty lie in usefulness or fitness or satisfaction of human desires ? Does it lie in mere rhythm or harmony or proportion? Does it reside in mere perfection of adjustment and adaptation? Is human beauty a mere *Maya* of the instinct of race-preservation? Is natural beauty a mere Maya of the instinct of self-preservation? How can we account in this way for our sense of beauty of the sun and moon and stars? Or is our love of Beauty due to a search by our spirit for the Absolute Beauty which had been realised by us in an anterior and purer state of existence? Or is Beauty the total of broken hints and suggestions and calls of the Divine Oversoul to the human soul? Where are we to search for the essence of beauty? What is it that lends such charm and attractiveness and fascination to beauty? Is beauty subjective or objective or both?

It is not possible to deal in this brief book with these subtle questions fully and thoroughly and to expound the views of all the western thinkers and writers on Beauty and Art and Aesthetics from Socrates to Croce. Some writers have stressed unity, symmetry, balance, and proportion as being the constituent factors of beauty. Some have stated that unity in diversity is the secret of beauty. Yet others have said that the vital element is order. Others have affirmed that rhythm is the essence. Some others have said that colour, form, brightness, expression and grace constitute beauty. Thinkers have differed also as to the interconnection of the true, the beautiful and the good. Are these diverse and divergent and disconnected or synthetic and connected and harmonious ?

It is no doubt true that such inquiries are not frequent in the eras of great creative activity. The joy of the creation of works of art as the result of a passionate realisation of the beautiful is so intense and absorbing that no time or energy is left over for aesthetic speculation. Great poets have also deprecated that self-dissection which seeks to analyse beauty. In a very beautiful stanza in the *Sakuntala* Kalidasa suggests this in his own inimitable manner and with his never-failing deftness and delicacy of touch. He makes Dushyanta address thus, in a most wonderful stanza where every word is expressive and suggestive, the bee that pursues Sakuntala and sings as it pursues and pursues as it sings:

चलापाङ्गां दृष्टिं स्पृशसि बहुशो वेपथुमतीं

रहस्याख्यायीव स्वनसि मृदु कर्णान्तिकचरः ।

करौ व्याधुन्वत्याः पिबसि रतिसर्वस्वमधरं
वयं तत्त्वान्वेषान्मधुकर हतास्त्वं खलु कृती ॥

(You touch often the tremulous eye whose side-long glances are so quick and changeful. You soar near her ears and sound sweetly there as if you whisper secrets of love in her ears. You taste her lips, which contain the quintessence of amorous delights, despite her deprecating hands. O honey-maker! we are undone by our search about the truth of things. You are the happy being as you seek bliss in preference to knowledge).

All the same when the tide of creative expression of Beauty ebbs, the human spirit pauses and seeks to know the source and nature of beauty. Who was the fleeting visitant? Whence came such angel-visits, few and far between? How much have such realisations added to the inner treasury of the human race? However much strict speculations on Aesthetics have differed in form and content in all times and climes,—have they not differed in the realms of Ethics and Metaphysics as well?—they show a vital unity and upwardness of surge.

Let us affirm once for all that beauty is as much a constituent of things as utility. Man never was or is or will be mere tongue or stomach. He is eye, ear, mind, heart, spirit as well. During the childhood of the race, the call of Beauty from the beauty of the heavens, from the beauty of the flowers and birds on earth, from the sweetness of perfumes and from the sweetness of the musical notes of the feathered creation charmed and fascinated and captivated and enraptured the heart of man. Man began to imitate Nature and ended by transcending Nature. Imitation was supplemented by decoration. Slowly came the contribution from the thrilled human heart. Its rich store of infinite love and wisdom and bliss brought from previous births and from its proximity to the Infinite Sacchidananda was contributed in a passion of giving as a love-offering. Once again I am anticipating and shall reserve this Indianness of outlook to a later chapter.

Egyptian art delighted in quantity and vastness and was characterised by an austere severity of outline. Hebrew art was dualistic and rejected pantheism and monism. The Hebrew race was ethical and not aesthetic or metaphysical in its bent. It is when we come to Greece, 'the mother of arts' that we see the elements of ease and freedom and lightness and rhythm and proportion and symmetry and grace. The Greeks had a keener sense of synthesis than the moderns, though it may be that they had not as keen a power of analysis. The Greeks shared in the monism of the Aryan vision of life but they had a keener sense of objective unity than of the unity of subject and object. Their great glory was that they realised and declared the unity of the True, the Beautiful, and the Good. They had a rare delicacy of perception and a keen sensitiveness and responsiveness to beauty. They had a fine and vigilant artistic sense, and concepts of symmetry and proportion and rhythm and order were inherent in their innermost nature. The serene and joyous and sunny clime of Greece reacted on an admirably-endowed and sensitive race. Greece was on the highway from the West to the East and received light from all quarters and radiated illumination abroad.

The Greek emphasis on gymnastics and music was not a mere accident. Their ideal was a sane and balanced mind in a healthy and beautiful body. Even their gods were humanised to the utmost extent. Greek speculation on Aesthetics is of great value as it influenced very considerably the modern theories of art and the modern works of art in Europe and America. Socrates declared that "whatever is beautiful is for the same reason good".

It was in Plato that aesthetic speculation in the West soared to the highest heights. According to him our love of beautiful things on earth is due to the search by our soul for the Absolute Beauty realised and enjoyed by us in an anterior and purer state of being. All visible things are types in which are mirrored the beauty of eternal archetypes. We must rise from the form to the idea, from the phenomenon to the noumenon. The following passages from his writings have become the classics of Aesthetic doctrine.

"He who would proceed aright in this matter should begin to visit beautiful forms ; Soon he will perceive that the beauty of one form is akin to the beauty of another ; and then, if beauty of form in general is his pursuit, how foolish would he be not to recognise that the beauty in every form is one and the same. And, when he perceives this, he will become a lover of all beautiful forms ; and next he will consider that the beauty of the mind is more honourable than the beauty of things onward." Plato then deals with the beauty of laws and sciences. He then says : "At length the vision will be revealed to him of a single science, which is the science of Beauty everywhere...a thing of wondrous beauty, which is ever ever-lasting, not growing and decaying, or waxing and waning......but beauty absolute, separate, simple and ever-lasting, which without diminution and without increase, is imparted to the ever-growing and perishing beauties of all other things... He learns to use the beauties of earth as steps along which he mounts upwards, going from fair forms to fair practices, and from fair practices to fair notions, until from fair notions he arrives at the notion of absolute Beauty, and at last knows what the esssence of Beauty is... If man has eyes to see the true beauty, he becomes the friend of God and immortal." (*Symposium.*)

Plato says in the *Phaedrus* that the Absolute Beauty is recognised as a supersensuous and spiritual essence which is discerned by the mind when thrown into ecstacy in its presence.

Aristotle did not recognise any absolute Beauty above and beyond the relative things which hint and express it. His was an analytical mind. He clearly demarcated the Beautiful from the Good. He however felt and saw that love of beauty is not like sense-desires which crave exclusive possession. The emotion of beauty is a disinterested emotion.

He says that order and symmetry are of the essence of beauty.

Plato's ideas were, however, adopted and developed by Plotinus and other Neo-Platonists. Plotinus declares that we realise the Eternal Beauty and Perfection not by generalisation from the actual but by direct intuition. He says: "That which sees must be kindred and similar to its object, before it can see it. The eye could never have beheld the sun, had it not become sun-like. The mind could never have perceived the beautiful, had it not first become beautiful itself. Every one must partake of the divine nature, before he can discern the divinely beautiful". The artist realises Eternal and Infinite Beauty and can hence create forms of beauty more beautiful than are found in the outer world. Beauty does not lie in mere symmetry of parts. It is a totality, a wholeness, a unity which is filled with the light invisible from transcendent Beauty and becomes permeated by the ethereal and delicate radiance of the mind.

I have thus indicated above the diversity and even irreconcilableness of the views of philosophers and aestheticians about the nature of beauty. I shall refer here to a few of the modern thinkers by way of illustration. Goethe said once : "Beauty is inexplicable; it is a hovering, floating and glittering shadow, whose outline eludes the grasp of definition". Schiller attributes beauty to the activity of the play-impulse. Schelling says that Art conducts us from the vestibule of Reality into the innermost shrine and reveals the transcendental to our vision. According to him art is its own authority. It is original and creative. Beauty, according to Hegel, is the disclosure of mind, or of the idea, through sensuous forms or media. Mind is higher than Nature, and therefore the beauty of Art is higher than the beauty of Nature. The works of art register man's visions of Beauty. A work of Art is not a mere nexus of lines, curves, forms, colours and kinds. Its value lies in the emotion or idea breathed into the work of art. The lustre of the idea, breaking down the barrier of the medium or materials illumines it with its light. Art is not a mirror of Nature. Art has Nature as its basis but its glory is in the palace built by it on such foundation. In architecture the material dominates. In sculpture art represents life and takes a step towards the ideal. In painting colour is added to form. In music the medium is the most tenuous of all and it is the most subjective of all the arts. Poetry deals with words which are spiritual and are charged with the ideas and feelings of ages. It is the most universal and spiritual of all the arts. Schopenhauer carries the idea of Hegel even further. According to him it is when desire ceases and our ego is at rest, that we reach eternity and beauty and perfection. He says: "A work of genius is not a thing of utility. To be useless is its very patent of noblity. It exists for itself alone."

I shall indicate here only the views of a few other Continental writers merely to show the varieties of aesthetic speculation in the West. Comte says that beauty is more than mere agreeableness and that physical beauty is attractive because it is a mirror of the spiritual which underlies it. Guizot states that sculpture deals with static states while painting can represent emotion and action. Joulfroy points out that the emotion of the beautiful is a disinterested emotion. He defines Beauty as "the expression of the Invisible by the natural signs which manifest it." Topffer says that God is Beauty and that our *ideas* of beauty are *attributes* of the divine. He declares that the Beautiful—which is the splendour of the

True—is the nature of God. Pictet says that beauty is a manifestation of the divine idea and that Nature *contains* it but does not *possess* it. He says: "Emanating as a pure ray from the Supreme Intelligence, this idea reveals itself in Nature; thence reflected by Art, it shines under a thousand different forms in the heart of humanity." Amiel says: "There is no repose except in the absolute, the infinite and the divine." He says again: "Heroism, ecstacy, love, enthusiasm wear a halo round the brow, for they are a setting free of the soul, which through them gains force to make its envelope transparent, and shine through upon all around it. Beauty is thus a phenomenon belonging to the spiritualisation of matter." Eugene Veron's *L' Ethetique* is an acute work but it is not of an illuminating quality. He defines Art as "the manifestation of emotion, obtaining external interpretation, now by expressive arrangements of line, form or colour, now by a series of gestures, sounds or words governed by peculiar rhythmical cadence." Guyau shows how the evolutionary doctrine of Herbert Spencer about beauty is imperfect and erroneous. While beauty does not exclude utility, its nature is in the will of man adjusting means to ends. It it not a parasite on the

2

plant of life but is its blossom. He says that science can never drive out art. It is no more possible to take our heart from the world than it is possible to drive out the world from our heart. All the theories of astronomy cannot prevent the sight of the infinite heavens from filling us with longing and yearning and mystery, a desire which is not satisfied by knowledge. There is always an eternal suggestion, consequently an eternal poetry. Guyau says: "Life, morality, science, art, religion,—there is, as I believe, an absolute unity between these things. Great and serious art is that which maintains and manifests this unity."

Such were the views of the greater aestheticians in Germany and France. In modern times Croce says that beauty is the expression of intuition; and that aesthetical pleasure is caused by the successful expression of beauty. He says further: "Art is independent both of science and of the useful and the moral." He says also: "The beauty of nature is the discovery of the human imagination." In another passage he says: "Art affirms itself as a manifestation of feeling and does not possess value save from its lyrical character and from the imprint of the artist's personality."

English thought on Aesthetics is not remarkable for originality or depth. Joseph Spence says that the essence of Beauty lies in colour, form, expression and grace. Hogarth finds it in fitness, variety, uniformity, simplicity, intricacy, and quantity. In his *Essay* on *the Sublime and the Beautiful* Burke, after treating about the elements of vastness, infinity etc., which are elements of sublimity, turns to the questions of proportion and fitness and says that these are not of the essence of beauty, and declares that the real elements of beauty are smallness of size, smoothness of surface, variety of outline in curves, delicacy, and brightness and softness of colour. This analysis is very imperfect. Beautiful objects need not necessarily be small. Even the angular and the rough may be beautiful, as in the case of crystals and mountain scenery. Coleridge finds the secret of beauty in unity and harmony and says that it results from a pre-established harmony between Nature and Man. Beauty does not depend on use or fitness or proportion. In an oyster, the shell is useful but not beautiful. The pearl, which is beautiful, is produced by a pathological condition of the oyster. Carlyle syas that in art "we discern Eternity looking through

Time, the God-like rendered visible." He says in two pregnant sentences :

"The Fine Arts divorcing themselves from Truth, are quite certain to fall mad, if they do not die."

"All real Art is the disimprisoned soul of Fact."

Ruskin linked art and beauty to life and soul. To him art is not only moral but divine, and morals are not only good and true but also beautiful. By disinterested love of beauty we become more ethical and social and spiritual. He says well: "Life without industry is sin, and industry without art is brutality." Ruskin's thought is not clear and cogent when he tries to express the real core of the beautiful. J. F. Seeley says in a valuable essay : "Art is one of the natural forms assumed by joy." He says that rhythm is the soul of Art. Herbert Spencer attributes art to the play-impulse. Aesthetic feelings are roused not by the uses of things but by the things themselves. Mr. J. A. Symonds says in a suggestive essay : "There is a beauty which is never found in Nature but which requires a working of human thought to elicit it from Nature ; a beauty not of parts and single persons, but of complex totalities, a beauty not of flesh and blood, but of mind, imagination, feeling. It is this synthetic, intellectual, spirit-penetrated beauty to which the arts aspire." Emerson has given us some suggestive ideas on Beauty and Art. He says: "Truth and goodness and beauty are but different faces of the same All." In his essay on the Oversoul: "From within or from behind, a light shines through us upon things, and makes us aware that we are nothing but the light is all." He says again: "The sensual man conforms thoughts to things; the poet conforms things to his thoughts." Mr. E. S. Dallas says in his *Poetics* that pleasure is the harmonious and unconscious activity of the soul. I may conclude this brief and galloping review of theories of Beauty and Art by quoting a passage from George Santayana's *Reason in Art*: "The artist, being a born lover of the good, a natural breeder of perfections, clings to his insight. If the world calls his accomplishments vain, he can, with better reason call vain the world's cumbrous instrumentalities, by which nothing clearly good is attained...He has moulded existence into the likeness of thought and lost himself in that ideal achievement which, so to speak, beckons all things into being."

I have discussed thus far the opinions of various thinkers of the past and the present on the subject of Beauty and Art and Aesthetics. I shall refer briefly to the suggestive indications of a very few great western poets on the matter, because the poets, being the high-priests in the shrine of Beauty, express Her glory better than philosophers, though they are not so clear and systematic in expositon as the latter are. Dante described the poet as "the scribe of Eternal Love." Goethe says: "Art is called Art, simply because it is not nature." Shakespeare says:

"The poet's eye, in a fine frenzy rolling,
Doth glance from heaven to earth, from earth to heaven;
And as imagination bodies forth
The forms of things unknown, the poet's pen
Turns them to shape and gives to airy nothing
A local habitation and a name."

He says again:

"O'er that art
Which you say adds to nature, is an art
That nature makes."

Pope says: "All Nature is but Art unknown to thee." Young says: "The course of Nature is the Art of God." Thomson sings:

"But who can paint
Like Nature? Can Imagination boast,
Amidst its gay creation, hues like hers?"

Wordsworth says:

"In such access of mind, in such high hour
Of visitation from the living god,
Thought was not; in enjoyment expired."

"Add
The Light that never was on sea or land,
The consecration and the poet's dream."

Shelley sings in *The Prometheus Unbound*:

"On a poet's lips I slept
Dreaming like a love adept
In the sound his breathing kept:
Nor seeks nor finds her mortal blisses
But feeds on the aerial kisses
Of shapes that haunt Thought's wildernesses.
He will watch from morn to gloom
The lake-reflected sun illume
The yellow bees in the ivy-bloom,
Nor heed nor care what thing they be.
But from these create he can
Forms more real than living man
Nurslings of immortality."

It is in Keats that we reach in the West the innermost core of beauty and art and aesthetics. In his Endymion he points out the link of love between the human soul and the goddess of beauty who is attained first in darkness and then in light. In his *Hyperion* he declares that it is the eternal law

"That first in Beauty shall be first in might."

In his Lamia he shows how the spirit of Imagination shrinks from the cold freezing gaze of fact. In his Ode to Psyche he says that though he cannot see Psyche he can and will recreate her in his imagination and in his poetry. In his *Ode to Nightingale* he shows how we can reach the Eternal Sweetness "on the viewless wings of poesy, though the dull brain perplexes and retards." In his *Ode On a Grecian Urn* he makes the significant affirmation that

"Beauty is Truth, True beauty: This is all
Ye know on earth and all ye need to know."

Lowell says :

"He gazed on all within him and without him,
He watched the flowing of Times steady tide,
And shapes of glory floated all about him
And whispered to him and he prophesied".

I have selected here a few of the declarations of great poets only to show that they have seen deeper than most philosophers into the inter-relations of the beauty of outer realm of nature and the inner realm of mind, the relations of both to the Eternal and Ineffable and Infinite glory and beauty of God, the respective and relative contributions of beauty from nature and from human imagination, and the real nature of the charm of Beauty and of artistic creation and of aesthetic delight.

I have thus far discussed aesthetic theories in the West in some detail. I shall now proceed to discuss a few connected topics relating to art and aesthetics. Realism and Romanticism are permanent human moods which are rooted in the ultimate and profound depths of the human mind. Realism is imitative ; romanticism or idealism is creative. There is of course an element of creation in realistic imitation because even in realistic art we have not mere photographic reproduction but a process of selection and recombination and refining. There is also an element of imitation in idealism and romantic creation because such creation is a projection and extension and refinement of the real world and is not and cannot be an absolutely different realm of facts and values. But in the realm of realism there is an emphasis on fidelity to the real world while in the realm of romanticism and idealism there is an element of fidelity to the inner creation of the soul. Aristotle expressed the former mood when he said that Art is Imitation. He however points out that the objects of imitation in Art is the Universal, not the Particular. Bacon expressed the latter mood when he said that in Art we have "the shows of things submitted to the desire of the mind." He said further that art pleases "by exhibiting an idea more grateful to the mind than the things themselves afford." If mere imitation of nature is of the essence of art, colour photography would be the finest painting. Mr. Burne-Jones, who is a great modern artist, says well: "Transcripts from Nature! What do I want with transcripts? I prefer her own signature. I don't want forgeries more or less skilful. It is the message, the 'burden' of a picture that makes its real value." Art can never fully imitate nature as nature is always changing. Collingwood says well in his *Philosophy of Art*: "To imagine is to isolate the object," Art focusses and renders static fragments of the real and the ideal and fills them with a new light from the glory of the soul. Thus Art should not merely imitate reality;

it should interpret, generalise, idealise and transfigure reality. It should touch and transfigure life.

The highest purpose of art is not in mere decoration but in expression. Decorative art aims at arranging lines, forms, colours, sounds and rhythms irrespective of the idea or sentiment. Expressive art aims at expressing the idea and the sentiment. The former works from without inwards; the latter works from within outwards. The former appeals primarily to the eye or the ear; the latter appeals primarily to the mind and the heart. It is in the latter that we reach and attain and enjoy the highest joy that Art can confer on the human heart.

It has been further said that art is due to the play impulse in man. A well-known verse in Bharata's Natya Sastra says 'क्रीडनीयकमिच्छामो दृश्यं श्रव्यं च यद्भवेत्' (We wish to have a sweet play-thing which can be seen and heard). This is another way of stating what has been well said in India that Art is the overflow of the Ananda (bliss of the soul) along the channels of perfect form. Man's duty is in work but his joy is in art. Tagore has well pointed out : "Essentially man is not a slave either of himself or of the world but he is a lover.

His freedom and fulfilment is in love which is another name for perfect comprehension." (*Sadhana*). Jesus expressed the same truth in perfect words when he said: "Consider the lilies of the field. They toil not neither do they spin. Yet even Solomon in all his glory is not arrayed like one of these." It has been well said that just as play is the art of the child, art is the play of the man. It is by becoming disinterested and wonder-filled and delighted at the sight of God's creation that man becomes fitted for the kingdom of art, just as he becomes fitted for the kingdom of God. Jesus says: "Verily I say unto you, except ye turn and become as little children, ye shall in no wise enter into the kingdom of heaven...Suffer the little children to come unto me and forbid them not: for of such is the kingdom of God. Verily I say unto you, whoever shall not receive the kingdom of God as a little child, he shall in no wise enter therein."

The law of Beauty does not in any way bar the expression and presentation of painful things. But it certainly requires that such expression and presentation should be true and beautiful and should be—to use Mathew Arnold's beautiful phrase—under the laws of poetic truth and poetic beauty. Niobe and Laocoon fills us with a pure and chastened delight. There is an aesthetic element in pain just as there is a spiritual element in pain. The former is the manifestation of the beauty of the soul through unfavourable surroundings, like the sun seen through a mist. The latter is the manifestation of the purity and blessedness of the soul through unfavourable surroundings. The crucifixion is thus the subject of a supreme aesthetic idealisation and expression and presentation as well as of a supreme spiritual realisation and expression and presentation. It seems to me that the aesthetic value of pain is not in mere perfection of expression but in such perfection being the meduim of manifestation of the beauty of the soul. Pain which is aesthetically expressed and realised quickens our finer impulses of compassion, sympathy, and love and sets free the soul from the prison of narrowness and selfishness and isolation.

In art expression is an end in itself. It is not a means to a further end. It is the beautiful expression of a realised aesthetic delight. But its purpose is the communication of such delight to others. Art is beauty refracted through the artist's mind to the world. The artist's delight is his own private ecstacy. But his artistic expression is for the uplift and rapture of humanity. His aesthetic mood is a rich compound of sensation and intellection and emotion and spiritual feeling and he kindles a kindred composite mood in others. His symbolic imagery is a means of creating a corresponding aesthetic feeling in others.

Idea as well as technique are vital elements in aesthetic expression. Technique is the symbolic vesture of the idea. It is the body of which the aesthetic idea is the soul. The body is diverse in each art as the medium of expression in each art is of a different character and as the density and plasticity of the artistic material differ from art to art. But it is the technique that gives us a sense of the coherence and interrelation and harmony and significance of the work of art.

In respect of the materials of aesthetic presentation, there are certain fundamental elements which form the basis of aesthetic pleasure. The straight line, the curve, and the circle are symbolical of certain fundamental things in life and raise different aesthetic perceptions and emotions. The straight line suggests and symbolises eternity. The curve suggests variety and gradation. The circle symbolises the finite. In the same way there are symbolism and suggestiveness in words and sounds. Further, the expressions of the grave and the gay in the human face certainly affect our conceptions and expressions of the grave and the gay in art. The smiling face has upward curving lines; the sorrowful face has downward curving lines. Life in repose and life in action suggest different curves and colours and harmonies and images.

Thus Art selects and fixes and refines the rarer and more radiant experiences and dreams of Beauty. But for the aid of the guardian angel such experiences and dreams will vanish into the void of nothingness. Not only will such realisations be lost to others; age and disease and even sheer forgetfulness will lead to their loss to the lucky and happy individual who experienced the joy of such realisations. Our reactions of delight during realisations of beauty of form or figure or tint or sound or thought should be conserved and immortalised and crowned with the unfading amaranthine flower of art. Our self-creations of delight in moods of perfect inner poise and peace and bliss should be equally and similarly conserved and expressed and immortalised.

In Art, and in art alone, next to religion and

philosophy, is the world realised and expressed as a unity and as a harmony. Its world is a congruous, coherent, significant world. No cruel discord shatters its inter-related unity, "its linked sweetness long-drawn out." It eliminates all dark patches of chance. Its perfection of form is but the outer radiant sheath of its significant creativeness of aesthetic mood. In short, beauty is the innermost essence of things. In actual life it is however marred by innumerable irrelevencies and incoherences. Art isolates the beauty of things and shows them as a cosmos of coherent and significant loveliness.

Art is thus a spontaneous expression of pure and essential human nature. It is static and dynamic. The static mood of art delights in order and proportion and simultaniety and results in the fine arts of architecture and sculpture and painting. The dynamic mood of art delights in movement and rhythm and succession and results in the fine arts of poetry and music and dancing. It is a subjective reaction on objective reality. It is never mere creation or mere imitation. It is a creative imitation rather than an imitative creation.

There is a hierarchy in art. Architecture and sculpture and painting are arts of repose and deal with space and appeal to the eye. Music and poetry are arts of movement and deal with time. Music appeals to the ear and Poetry appeals to the mind. They are more intimate in their appeal to the soul than the other arts. Regularity in space is form. Regularity in time is rhythm. Of the media of art the medium of architecture and sculpture is the least plastic of all. The medium of painting is more plastic. The medium of Music is sound which is the most plastic and subtle of all the media of Art. But the medium of poetry is the most spiritual and powerful of all the media of Art. It is language which is the incarnate thought of man and consists of words which have come to us charged with the thoughts and emotions of generations. Poetry is architectonic like architecture, statuesque like sculpture, graphic and picturesque like painting and rhythmical like music and is yet something beyond and above them all.

The dance arose as an art in the desire for the physical expression of emotions. It is the poetry of movement and gesture. Music arose from the desire for the vocal expression of emotions. Music is the dance of words and dance is the music of the human limbs. Sculpture and painting arose from the desire for the imitation of Nature. Of them painting had a more plastic and expressive medium than sculpture. It has been well said that architecture arose as a fact and developed into an art. It began as a physical want and became a psychical manifestation. Architecture and sculpture aud painting appeal primarily to the eye while music appeals primarily to the ear. But as shown above it is in poetry that we have the queen of all arts. It appeals to the mind which is the queen of the senses. Thus of all the arts poetry alone has the glorious privelege of appealing directly to the mind. But form, rhythm, metre, imagery, etc., are also of the utmost importance in poetry. Its medium is the human language which is the most subtle and expressive of all the media of artistic expression. The arts that appeal to the eye can present only a single moment of time. Music can express only a small number of passions. Even these must be universal and cannot have the variety of individuality. Poetry is inferior to each of the other arts in its special method of expression. But it includes them all and transcends them. Its domain has no rigid boundaries of any sort.

The poet's main glory is his power of pictorial expression. A picture is beauty bathed in the light of emotion ; a symbol is beauty bathed in the light of the intellect. Even the matter-of-fact truths of science shine out as pictures in the golden frame of the poet's imaginations. Intuition, vision and expression unite and shine forth in true and authentic poetry. These are inborn gifts. *Poeta nascitur non fit.* "All that education can give a poet is experience and a vocabulary." Enormous condensation converts carbon into diamond; even so in poesy. Thus the brilliance of poetic expression is partly due to pictorial power and partly due to its being the best and briefest words in the best order. The true poet makes a new and fresh use of old and simple words; he puts life into them and gives them wings. The shining hues of imagination harmonise with the shining hues of expression.

Poetry must further be a criticism and interpretation of life. It is however not mere criticism of life; it is a revelation of super-life through such criticism of life. It is life ideally realised and emotionally and imaginatively presented. It speaks to the heart and the imagination and thereby refines our intellect and sweetens our will. But its primary appeal is to the heart and not to the intellect or the will. Dryden says well: 'Poetry only instructs as it delights.'

I shall now proceed to deal briefly with the various fine arts and their achievements in the West in brief detail. Mr. R. A Freeman refers in his work on *Social Decay and Regeneration* "to the fundamental aesthetic truth that the work of every craft should be dominated by the genius of the material and that of the appropriate tool and process." Of all the fine arts the mother art is certainly architecture. Savage man lived in caves and forests. But as soon as he knew how to use implements, he scooped out artificial caves and began to live there. Later on he learnt how to work wood in such a way as to afford him shelter. It is probable that the Gothic or pointed style of architecture sprang from the fact that the Gauls generally used wood for their buildings. The use of granite in South Indian temple buildings largely determined the forms of South Indian architecture. The houses of gods were fashioned on a more vaster and grandiose scale than in the case of private dwellings. Only then architecture rose from an industry into an art. It rose from utility to beauty. Men aimed at combining size and vastness with ornamentation and decorative sign. Their imagination took wings when agriculture freed them from old perpetual hunt for food. In fact and in short agriculture led to architecture and architecture led to the other arts.

In Greece we see the Doric, Ionic and Corinthian styles. In Greek architecture we find a system determined by mathematical calculations. We find a predominance of straight lines in it. It excels in the harmony of the parts resulting in the production of the desired aesthetic effect.

Roman architecture was imitative of Greek architecture but the Romans were the first to understand the value of the keyed arch, which was originally discovered in the Orient. The keyed arch accomodates itself to all materials.

The originality of the Byzantine architecture is in bold domes. It borrowed the column from Greece and the arch and the vault from Rome.

The Saracenic style uses columns to support arches and rests domes upon pendentives disposed in square. We find within the structure a refined profusion of ornamentation. But in this ornament, every sort of animal representation is excluded. It depends for effect upon variety of lines and forms and colours. But it does not present to us any richness of idea.

In the Romanesque style we find the combination of the Roman basilica and a transverse nave. This was done to give the edifice the form of a cross.

In the Gothic style we find the pointed arch. This enabled men to construct churches which were lighter and higher than before. Thus height began to dominate over size. As the weight of the roof was rested upon the flying buttress, the builders were able to replace the wall to a large extent by stained glass windows. Thus a new accessory art *viz.*, the art of painting on glass took its birth and added to architectural loveliness and effect. Thus the new style had more freedom and elasticity than the older styles.

But architecture is the least free of the arts. It is never entirely free from the fetters of utility. It is dependent largely on materials, climate, light, and habits. But within such limitations it has its own wonders of artistic expressiveness. Horizontal lines leave the impression of stability, and durability, while vertical lines express boldness and aspiration. Plain surfaces suggest austerity. Ornamentation suggests gaiety.

The real aim of sculpture was to make real to the eye the forms of the gods. But side by side with such symbolic sculpture, we find also the development of natural and human sculpture. Thus religious as well as realistic sculpture has flourished in the world.

Sculpture in Greece excelled in both the above respects. Religious sculpture attained its culmination there in Phidias. His work marks the high water-mark of achievement in beauty, symmetry, repose and expressiveness.

M. Vernon says: "Above physical beauty—which chiefly exists in just proportions, in the adaptation of means to end, of organ to function, in the happy arrangement of line and form— there is another kind of beauty, which is the exterior expression of the power to feel and comprehend. Antique sculpture never got beyond the lower of these excellences, except in the case of a small number of artists who attempted to add to it the expression of some of the more exterior and easily rendered sentiments. The modern sculptor following the example set by Michael Angelo, is less preoccupied with phsyical perfection than with moral perfection."

Architecture and sculpture appeal to two of our senses—the eye and the touch. But painting appeals to the eye alone. Perspective and colour are its vital elements. Colour leads to distinction of objects. Perspective creates the illusion of space. *Chiaroscuro* means the arrangement of light and shade while colour is the arrangement of colours other than black and white. It is by chiaroscuro and perspective that the painter indicates various planes. The architect and the sculptor cannot control light and shade but the painter can and does. Delicacies of touch and tone are also added by him to delicacies of tint and perspective. The achievements of great painters in the West and especially in Italy are wonderful in variety and charm. They were not only makers of beautiful things but were seers and men of vision. They excelled in all varieties of the art *viz.*, landscape painting, painting of human forms, and painting of spiritual themes.

Music has a great variety of manifestation in the world. The Negroes have but four notes. The Chinese have five notes. In India melody predominates. In Europe harmony is dominant. But all music is an adventure in the realm of sounds. Herbert Spencer has proved how variations in the voice are the physiological results of changes in the singer's feelings. In the ear the three thousand fibres terminating in the filaments of the acoustic nerve are like three thousand strings. But the mainspring of music is neither in voice nor in ear but in feeling. It serves no materialistic purposes and is hence not connected with the utilities of life. It copies nothing and is hence not mere imitative but is gloriously creative. Just as Greece excels in sculpture and Italy excels in painting, Germany excels in music. The great compositions of Wagner and Mendelssohn and Mozart and Beethoven show the finest achievements of the West in the subtlest and sweetest of all the arts.

I shall say little here about the fine arts of poetry and drama because my main purpose in this work is to deal with aesthetics. Throughout the world the finest flowering of art is in poetry and drama. In the West poetry and drama have felt the pressure of aesthetic theories from time to time. Classic poetry and drama had a severe simplicity of outline. Modern poetry and drama have been emancipated from the mediaeval obsession with the religious life and are dominated by the Hellenic spirit as intensified by the modern realistic and scientific spirit. The result is that modern poetry and drama are as varied and many-sided and intricate and complicated as modern life itself. They aim at the pourtrayal of life in its totality but their exclusive concentration on the theory that "the proper study of mankind is man" has led to their loss of interest in the eternal verities of the spirit and has resulted in a thinning of the spiritual content of their achievement.

I shall say a few words here about the art of acting because without its aid the art of drama can never achieve its full effect. The actor's contribution of personality is his greatest contribution to the play. In the modern drama, the partnership in imagination of author and actor and audience is the real secret of dramatic success. Dancing and music have deserted the drama and have set up their own booths as ballet and opera. The drama has gained rather than lost by such defection of an ancient partnership. It has well been said that "four boards and a passion are all the equipment that drama needs." Though plot and incidents are of the essence of drama, it is the representation and exhibition of human character that is its inmost essence. Such representation of character requires the co-operation, of the actor with the author. Indeed without the actor's part in such vivid representation a drama will have but a half-dead life.

The illusion of reality is zealously pursued on the modern stage. As has been said well: "By the old method the stage and the actor were brought into the midst of the audience, by the new the audience is lured in imagination on the stage." The realistic setting has been perfected. If to it is added realism of character-representation the effect becomes electrical. Objective truth is but the body of dramatic power, its soul is subjective truth. Scenic symbolism is of value; but of very greater value is the interpretation of passion—of dynamic emotion by dynamic speech.

In concluding this chapter I shall say a few words on the question of taste. Taste is diverse and variable, but its essential characteristic is that it is the capacity to feel aesthetic pleasure. It implies a fine sensitiveness to lines and colours and sounds and words and ideas. It implies a grasp of the congruousness of things and ideas and forms. It has been well said that it is "the faculty possessed by a true artist, to seize by a kind of intuition, the fitting relation of things, whether in works as a whole, or in their details."

But there is a difference between the taste of artist the taste of the critic and the taste of the ordinary man. The taste of the artist is primary, synthetic, and of the essence of creative delight. The taste of the critic is secondary, analytic and of the essence of revelatory pleasure. The taste of the man in the street is tertiary, receptive and of the essence of perceptive sensibility. Without a synthetic and concrete and creative power of a high order there can be no artistic genius. Without an analytic and abstract and critical power of a high order there can be no critic of genius. Without a cultured and trained and keen power of aesthetic discernment there cannot be that fine specimen of humanity—the man of taste. On him more than on even the artist and the critic depend the well-being of Art and Aesthetics.

CHAPTER II.

The Differentia Of Indian Aesthetics.

THIS is a subject on which there is a great deal of dense ignorance even in India, and quite naturally there is a great deal of even denser ignorance in the West. Professor Knight in his valuable work on *The Philosophy of the Beautiful* says: "In the earlier times, the sense of Beauty slumbered, as it did in India, and amongst the Aryan races generally. It is perhaps the more remarkable that it should not have awakened earlier in India, when we remember that almost all the distinctive types of philosophical thought had sprung up, that a monistic as well as a dualistic conception of the world prevailed alongside of the popular polytheism and nature-worship. But there is scarcely a trace of a feeling for the beautiful in the Brahminical or Buddhist writings." Mr. Vincent Smith says that the inhabitants of India have always been "singularly indifferent to aesthetic merit and little qualified to distinguish between good and bad art."

Such ignorance of the truth about Indian Aesthetics by western professors is hardly remarkable when we remember that no less than a reputed *savant* like Professor Max Muller stated: "The question which you ask has occupied my mind for many years. I remember Humboldt, when he was writing his Kosmos, asking me what the Indians thought of the Beautiful in Nature. I gave him several descriptions of Nature, which I believe he published, but I had to tell him *that the idea of the Beautiful in Nature did not exist in the Hindu mind.* It is the same with their descriptions of human beauty. They describe what they saw, they praise certain features; they compare them with other features in Nature; but the Beautiful as such does not exist for them. *They never excelled either in sculpture or painting.* Their sculpture is meant to express thought, and they do not mind giving a god ever so many arms to indicate his omnipotence. When painting comes in they simply admire its mirroring and life-likeness. With regard to actions, again, they speak of them as good or bad, brave or mean, but never as simply beautiful......It would be quite impossible to render *Tokalon* in Sanskrit. Beautiful, *Sobhana*, means bright; *pesala*, variegated *ramaniya*, pleasant. The beauty of poetry is expressed by *madhuni* the sweet things; the beauty of nature by *sobah*, splendour. Of course there is a goddess of beauty Sri and Lakshmi, but they are both late and they represent happiness rather than simple beauty. Even this negative evidence may be useful as showing what is essential for the development of the concept of the Beautiful. But it is strange nevertheless, that a people so fond of the highest abstractions as the Hindus, should never have summarised their perceptions of the Beautiful."

Such is the dense ignorance of even the learned about the Indian Aesthetics. It is strange—to use Max Muller's words—that persons so fond of the Indians and so learned in Indian lore like Max Muller should never have known and enjoyed the Indian concepts of Beauty and Art and Aesthetics. Since his time the treasury of Indian literature on Aesthetics has been opened to all. Dr. Ananda Comarasamy has spent a life-time in making the world aware of the significance of Indian art. Rabindranath Tagore has rewon the homage of the world to Indian poesy. The Bengali school of Art has carried forward the great artistic tradition and achievements of the past of India into India's future. But as yet clear notions do not obtain in India or elsewhere about the aesthetic concepts and theories and achievements into the Indian genius.

The Indian mind which is admittedly gifted with penetrating speculative powers, could certainly not have been barren in aesthetic speculation. I shall show later how its fundamental aesthetic concepts have influenced profoundly the development of Indian Art. I am concerned here with the demonstration of the radiant existence of a Philosophy of the Beautiful in India and of the value of Indian aesthetic concepts.

The most fundamental of aesthetic concepts—just as it is the most fundamental of spiritual concepts—is *Ananda* (Bliss). That bliss is the innermost core of being has been affirmed again and again by Indian aestheticians as by Indian philosophers.

आनन्दो ब्रह्मेति व्यजानात् । आनन्दाद्ध्येव खल्विमानि भूतानि जायन्ते । आनन्देन जातानि जीवन्ति । आनन्दं प्रयन्त्यभिसंविशन्तीति ।

(He knew Brahma as Ananda. All living beings are born from Ananda. Having been born they live in and by Ananda. They move onwards towards and enter Ananda). Taittiriya Upanishad, III, 6.

आनन्दं ब्रह्मणो विद्वान्न बिभेति कुतश्चनेति ।

(Knowing Brahma to be Ananda, he casteth out fear)
Taittiriya Upanishad, II, 9.

The Taittiriya Upanishad takes us into further depths of this blissful core of being.

तस्माद्वा एतस्माद्विज्ञानमयात् अन्योऽन्तर आनन्दमयः । तस्य प्रियमेव शिरः । मोदो दक्षिणः पक्षः । प्रमोद उत्तरः पक्षः । आनन्द आत्मा । ब्रह्मपुच्छं प्रतिष्ठा ।

(Even subtler than the element of intellection is the element of bliss. Of it the joy or *priya* caused by the *experience* of beautiful and enjoyable things is the head. The finer joy or *moda* (caused by the *enjoyment* of beautiful and enjoyable things) is the right wing. The intenser joy or *pramoda* (caused by the *expression* of beautiful and enjoyable things) is the left wing. The element of bliss which is the common constituent of *priya*, *moda*, and *pramoda* is its Atma or soul. Brahma the Oversoul is its eternal basis and sustaining support). (The italics are mine), Taittiriya Upanishad II, 5.

The very same idea, with the aid of the same simile, is expressed by Keats when he sings in his *Ode to the Nightingale*.

"Away ! away ! for I shall fly to thee,
Not charioted by Bacchus and his pards
But on the viewless wings of poesy
Though the dull brain perplexes and retards."

This is not all. The aesthetic concept of Ananda and the spiritual concept of Ananda are so brought together that we are able to realise their inter-relation in a manner which western thought has never known. Even today aestheticians and moralists are fighting in the West about the ethical value of art and about the moral indifference of art. There is the old cry—raised again and again—about 'art for art's sake'. In the Taittiriya Upanishad (II, 8) we have a vivid description of an ascending grade of bliss. Then follows the declaration that all these levels of bliss are comprised and transcended in the bliss of the sinless and passionless saint. The joy of the artist is but one of the levels of human bliss though it is higher than mere material enjoyment. It must know its place and realise the supremacy of the bliss of sinlessness and saintliness.

I must desist from working out this concept or the next concept here farther lest this work should swell to undue proportions. I shall now briefly refer to the concept of Rasa and advert to the inter-relations between Indian aesthetics and Indian metaphysics in the last chapter. What I am aiming at in these chapters is to show that the Indians have always had a noble and beautiful philosophy of the Beautiful and general concepts of Beauty and Art and Aesthetics.

The next aesthetic concept to be considered is that of *Rasa*. This is the most fundamental of all the concepts worked out in our great books on Aesthetics. I am devoting a special chapter to it below. I am referring to it also in the last chapter because the concepts of Ananda and Rasa are fundamental ideas in Indian Metaphysics as well as in Indian Aesthetics. Mammata brings the two concepts together thus in his famous *Kavya Prakasa* सकलप्रयोजनमौलिभूतं समनन्तरमेव रसास्वादनसमुद्भूतं विगलितवेद्यान्तरमानन्दम् ।

(Joy which is the crown of all the aims of life, which is immediately produced by the relish of Rasa and which so fills the mind that one is aware of nothing else).

In the Taittiriya Upanishad we have the famous declaration

रसो वैसः रसं ह्येवायं लब्ध्वाऽनन्दी भवति । (II, 7)

(He is Rasa having obtained Him the soul becomes full of bliss).

Rasa is in fact that aesthetic perception and

enjoyment of the beautiful which is related to Beauty on the one side and Art on the other. Bhartrihari says in a well-known stanza:—

जयति ते सुकृतिनो रससिद्धाः कवीश्वराः (II. 24.)

(The poets who are pure and are masters of *Rasa* are triumphant in the world).

By a peculiar linguistic fortune the word indicates not only god and aesthetic delight but alchemy and the elixir of life as well. Thus aesthetic enjoyment transforms the lead of life into gold, enables us to realise our real immortality as an enjoyer of aesthetic (as distinguished from sensuous) bliss, and leads us to spiritual bliss. Thus we get the elements of value, beauty, immortality and spirituality in aesthetic enjoyment. Aesthetic delight is different from the pleasure of utility; it is enjoyable by human beings during all stages of existence; it is disinterested and unselfish and sinless and pure; it gives an extension to our personality; it gives a new intensity to it; and it trains the restless mind to lose itself in the joy of art so that in course of time it may lose itself in spiritual bliss.

The general concept of Beauty is expressed by the word *Soundarya* (the Beautiful) or *Ramaniya*-

ta (the Attractive) or *charuta* (the Lovely and Handsome). In this concept we have three important and illuminative elements. There is an attempt made in the following verse to express the very core of beauty.

क्षणे क्षणे यन्नवतामुपैति तदेव रूपं रमणीयतायाः ।

(The very essence of Beauty lies in its power of revealing new aspects every instant and holding our attention and admiration by its ever-new attractiveness).

Just as when we take a cut diamond or shot silk into the sunlight, every turning of the gem or the silk in our hands reveals new and radiant and coruscating splendours, even so the really beautiful thing or idea defies analysis and is full of ever-new radiance.

The second element is the element of reminiscence which is due to our previous experience of beauty in other births. Kalidasa brings out this aspect in a famous stanza in his *Sakuntala*.

रम्याणि वीक्ष्य मधुरांश्च निशम्य शब्दान्
पर्युत्सुकी भवति यत् सुखितोऽपि जन्तुः ।
तच्चेतसा स्मरति नूनमबोधपूर्वं
भावस्थिराणि जननान्तरसौहृदानि ॥

(The reason why, on seeing beautiful objects and hearing harmonious sounds, even a happy man becomes full of longing and melancholy is that he remembers, without the experience rising to the surface of the working consciousness, the companionships and enjoyments which he had in previous births and which are an integral portion of his treasury of emotion).

The very same idea is expressed by D. G. Rossetti when he says in the *House of Life* :

"O born with me somewhere that men forget
And though in years of sight and sound unmet
Known for my soul's birth-partner well enough."

The third element is the fact that all beauty on earth is but a glimpse of the Absolute and Infinite Beauty of God, the attainment of which is the secret and eternal longing of the human soul. God has been well described by Sri Madhusudana Sarasvati as *Soundarya Sara Sarvasva* (the supreme treasure of the essence of Beauty). That the expression of the greatness and glory and beauty and love and grace of God is a higher function of Art than even the expression of natural beauty and human beauty and that it fulfils even better the real function of art as an ever-new revealer of ever-new loveliness and an ever-generous giver of mental delight and an ever-efficient dispeller of grief and sorrow and pain in this vale of tears "where beauty cannot keep her lustrous eyes nor new love pine at them beyond tomorrow" is clear from the well-known stanza in the Srimad Bhagavata:

> तदेव रम्यं रुचिरं नवं नवं
> तदेव शश्वन्मनसो महोत्सवम् ।
> तदेव शोकार्णवशोषणं नृणां
> यदुत्तमश्लोकयशोऽनुगीयते ॥

(The singing of the glory of God is the revealing of ever-new and ever-radiant Beauty, the bestowal of eternal and matchless bliss on the heart, and the destroyer of the engulfing ocean of human grief and sorrow and pain).

Indian aestheticians are not oblivious of the elements of rhythm, harmony, proportion, order, symmetry, balance, unity in variety, colour, form, brightness, grace, etc., in beauty. In fact in describing Sri Rama as an incarnation of aesthetic as well as ethical loveliness, Valmiki describes him as *dyutiman* (bright), *samavibhaktanga* (of symmeterical form), *snigdhavarna* (of fascinating colour), *subhalakshana* (having auspicious expressiveness) etc. But the Indian aestheticians have specially stressed the above three elements—the element of ever-new self-revelation, the element of reminiscence of ante-natal experience and enjoyment and expression, and the element of kinship to the supreme and eternal and infinite beauty of God.

I now proceed to deal briefly with the concept of Art (Kala). Art is the expression of Beauty just as Beauty is the expression of Ananda. In respect of Art three elements clearly stand out in the Indian concept—creativeness, sweetness, and spiritual devotion. I shall refer very briefly to these concepts here. A well-known verse in the *Dhvanyaloka* says :

अपारे काव्यसंसारे कविरेव प्रजापतिः ।
यथास्मै रोचते विश्वं तथैवेतत्प्रवर्तते ॥

(In the limitless world of the poet's creation, the poet is himself the creator. It lives and moves and has its being as it pleases him).

In Mammata's *Kavya Prakasa* there occurs the following famous stanza.

नियतिकृतनियमरहितां
ह्लादैकमयीमनन्यपरतन्त्रां
नवरसरुचिरां निर्मितिमा-
दधती भारतीकवेर्जयति ॥

(The poet's speech creates a world which is not fettered by the laws of Destiny, which is of the very essence of joy, which is self-existent and not dependant on anything else, and which brings into being a creation shining with the nine rasas).

Thus the Indian aestheticians declare beyond doubt that creativeness is of the essence of Art.

That beauty and grace and sweetness are of the essence of Art has been proclaimed by Sanskrit rhetoricians by an idea very familiar to students of Indian literature. The method of the scriptural teaching is the mode of a royal edict. (*Prabhu sammita*). Its teaching is a command. Our duty is to obey and in the case of the command the joy is in the fruit and not in the process. The method of the *Puranas* (ethical stories) is the method of a comrade, *Suhrit-Sammita*). His words do not cause fear like a royal command but result in joy if we follow them. He persuades, appeals, illustrates and demonstrates the truth. The method of poesy is that of a lovely and beloved and graceful and gracious wife *Kanta Sammita*). The promulgation, the process and the goal of the teaching by her are equally sweet and attractive and full of joy. All the three attitudes of the soul in relation to Truth are referred to in the grand verse in Chapter XI of the Gita : "पितेव पुत्रस्य सखेव सख्युः प्रियः प्रियायार्हसि देव सोढुम्"

The artist is a seer. Sri Sankaracharya interprets kavi (poet) as meaning *krantadarsi* (one who sees far and wide and deep and knows the truth of things). The artist feels and sees the Eternal Beauty in his most exalted and entranced moods and spends his less exalted moments in the visioning and expression of his realisations. His mind is a psychic radium and gives light undiminished and for ever. In him the tree of life is in a state of perpetual blossoming. This ideal of poesy wherein song and self-realisation become one in joy is of the essence of Indian conception of the real mission and value of art. Thus in India alone is found that golden link between devotion and love—devotion iridiscent with the prismatic colours of love and love lit up by the white light of devotion. Art is the perfume, and religion is the camphor, lighted in our worship of God.

Such is the concept of Art in India. The concept of Aesthetics is a natural evolution of the concepts of Beauty and of Art. The name given to the science of aesthetics is *Alamkara Sastra* or *Sahitya Sastra.* These two words express two aspects of aesthetics. One word expresses the idea that it is the science of the beautiful expression of the Beautiful. The other word expresses the idea that the science of the expression of Beauty is the true companion of our soul. *Sahitya* is not merely the union of word and sense in poetry, the union of sound and emotion in music, the union of colour and idea in painting, the union of beauty and repose in sculpture, and the union of beauty and vastness in architecture but it is also and essentially the union of beauty and bliss—the beauty of art and the bliss of the soul.

The aesthetic concept of *Taste* is equally valuable. All the books on Aesthetics in India emphasise the importance of the *Rasika* or the *Sahridaya* (the man of taste or the man of kindred aesthetic mood). Unless we have a large number of such persons of trained taste, the voice of art will be but a cry in the wilderness. It is on the man of taste that the well-being of Art and Aesthetics depends.

CHAPTER III.

The History of Indian Aesthetios.

IT is thus clear that Indian Aesthetics like Indian Art has got its valuable special features. In short the special features of Indian Aesthetics were derived from the special features of Indian Art and Indian Religion. The Veda is the common source of all of them. Its concepts of *rasa* and *ananda* have profoundly influenced not only Indian spirituality but also Indian poesy and Indian poetics as well. In the Brihadaranyaka Upanished the following simile occurs: 'तद्यथा प्रियया स्त्रिया संपरिष्वक्तो न बाह्यं किंचन वेद नान्तरम्'

(Just as a man who is held in close embrace by a beloved woman knows not what is within him or without him but is absorbed in bliss).

What is this compared to ?

एवमेवायं पुरुषः प्राज्ञेनात्मना संपरिष्वक्तो न बाह्यं किंचन वेद नान्तरं तद्वा अस्यै तदाप्तकाममात्मकाममकामं रूपं शोकान्तरम् ॥

(Even so the soul in union with the Oversoul knows not what is within or without. This realisation is the fullness of bliss, the bliss of the soul, the bliss of dispassion, and the utter negation of all grief and misery and pain and unhappiness).

The Veda contains not only the germ of the aesthetic concept but also the germs of Indian poetry and drama as well. The Ushas hymns and other hymns in the Rig Veda, the songs of the Sama Veda, and the passages about Brahman and Atman in the Upanishads contain the basic poetic ideas that fructified abundantly in later Indian poetry. The charming dialogues in the Vedas and especially in the Rig Veda and the Upanishads are the seeds of the later Indian drama.

Though *Alamkara Sastra* has a history of over a thousand years behind it, we do not see, and can hardly expect to see, its efflorescence in the *Veda*, though we certainly see its germ there as shown above. Poetics usually succeed Poesy all over the world : and this is a natural order. Yaska's *Nirukta* refers to Upama as used in the Vedas. Nighantu also refers to the particles of comparison relating to the Upama as used in the Veda. The Vedanta Sutras refer to *Upama* and *Rupaka* (see III, 2, 18 and I, 4. 1). Panini uses Upama, aupamya etc. In the Mahabhashya Patanjali illustrates the matter further and says that *mana* is measure and that *upamana* is what is near or approximate to a thing and makes us realise the thing not absolutely but relatively and approximately. These are all dry discussions devoid of emphasis on that element of delectable charm which is of the essence of aesthetics and aesthetic expression according to the exposition by later rhetoricians. The philosophical theories about the nature of Ananda have however a greater value and application in relation to the essence of Aesthetics. As stated already "*Rasa*" is equally applicable to God and to the soul of Art. As God is infinite Ananda, art is a bright ray from the sun of such Ananda.

Even more than the Vedas, the *Itihasas* (Ramayana and Mahabharata), the Puranas and especially the Bhagavata became the sources of Indian poetry and plays. They were also the sources of Indian poetics as well. Anandavardhana and Mammata rejoice in choosing stanzas from them as illustrations for their great and famous works on Aesthetics. The Mahabharata states about itself that it is the source of poetic stimulus to poets.

इतिहासोत्तमादस्माज्जायन्ते कविबुद्धयः ॥

(Adiparva, II, 385)

इदं कवि वरैः सर्वैराख्यानमुपजीव्यते ।

(Do. II, 389)

The Ramayana is the later poets' treasure-chamber, and Valmiki is the poet's poet. Bhoja says about Valmiki in his *Champuramayana* :

शुभमतनुत काव्यं स्वादु रामायणाख्यम् ।
मधुमयभणितीनां मार्गदर्शी महर्षिः ॥

(The great sage, who was the guide of all the sweet-tongued poets, composed the pure and auspicious and sweet poem called the Ramayana).

The *Dasarupaka* of Dhananjaya advises the poets and playwrights to go to the Ramayana and the Brihatkatha for their stories and plots.

Among the Puranas, the Agni Purana contains an elaborate description of the various Indian aesthetic concepts. It refers to Bharata. It discusses many figures of speech and even discusses the concept of *dhvani*. It is not possible to fix its date with any degree of certainty.

The systematic development of Indian Aesthetics went on for nearly two thousand years from before the beginning of the Christian era to the 18th century A. D., if we leave aside its unknown beginnings and sporadic early manifestations and confine our attention mainly to the period of its clear and continuous growth from Bharata to Jagannatha and Appayya

Dikshita. The most conspicuous contribution to the literature on Aesthetics was certainly that of the Kashmiri writers such as Anandavardhana and Mammata.

Nandikesvara is generally referred to as the progenitor and patron God of Aesthetics just as Hanuman and Narada are said to be the progenitors and patron Gods of Music. Rajasekhara's Kavyamimamsa makes Siva Himself the founder and teacher of Aesthetics. Kasyapa and Vararuchi are said to have left works on Aesthetics. But no such works are extant now. The earliest regular treatise is Bharata's *Natya Sastra*. Its date is unknown but it cannot be much later than the beginning of the Christian era. Kalidasa refers to Bharata in his Vikramorvasiya (मुनिना भरतेन यः प्रयोगो भवतीष्वष्टरसाश्रयः प्रयुक्तः). In my work an Kalidasa I shall show how the great poet was not later than the 1st century B. C.

I shall mention in this chapter only the great Indian writers on Aesthetics in their chronological order as I am discussing their views in the next chapter. Rajasekhara, at page 14 of his *Kavyamimamsa* (Gaekwad's Oriental Series), refers to Kalidasa himself as a writer on aesthetics. But no such work by Kalidasa is now extant.

Bhatti may be said to belong to the 5th century A. D. The tenth canto of his *Bhattikavya* is called Prasanna Kanda and contains illustrations of thirty-eight *alamkaras* or figures of speech.

The next great figure in the history of Indian Aesthetics is Bhamaha, the author of *Kavyalankara*. His work was known only from quotations for a long time. But recently Mr. Trivedi published it as an appendix to his edition of *Prarataparudrayaso-bhushana* and Mr. P. V. Naganatha Sastrigal of Tanjore is bringing out a critical edition of it. Bhamaha is the founder of the *Alamkara* theory. A keen controversy has been going on for many years past as to who was the earlier—Bhamaha or Dandin. It is one of the unsettled points of Indian chronology. There are many identical passages found in the works of both. Dandin is in affinity with the Bharata school while Bhamaha's school is a departure from that school. Both belong to the 5th or 6th century A. D. Bhamaha's *Kavyalankara* and Dandin's *Kavyadarsa* are among the greatest of the Indian works on Aesthetics.

Udbhata's *Alankarasara sangraha* is a work of great merit. He flourished about 800 A. D. and was an official in the Court of King Jayadeva of

Kashmir (779—813 A. D.) He deals with forty-one figures of speech. His illustrations are taken from his own poem *Kumara Sambhava* which is now lost. The commentary of *Pratiharenduraja* on Udbhata's work is of great value.

Vamana is another well-known writer on Aesthetics. His *Kavyalankara Sutra* contains his aphorisms (Sutras) and his *Vritti* (exposition) of aesthetics. He affirmed that *Riti* (style) is the soul of poesy (रीतिरात्मा काव्यस्य विशिष्टापदरचनारीतिः विशेषो गुणात्मा । and was thus the protagonist of the Riti school of Aesthetics. He belonged to the 8th century A. D. He is referred to in Rajasekhara's Kavyamimamsa. Abhinavagupta, the author of *Lochana* (the famous commentary on *Dhvanyaloka*), says that the Dhvanyaloka discusses Vamana's view. Ananda Vardhana, the author of *Dhvanyaloka*, belonged to the 8th century A. D. Vamana quotes from Bhavabhuti who belonged to the 7th century A. D.

Rudrata's *Kavyalankara* is a work of some merit. He belonged to 9th century and was a native of Kashmir. A keen controversy has been going on as to whether he is identical with Rudrabhatta, the author of Sringaratilaka. The balance of opinion is in favour of holding Rudrabhatta to be a different person and assigning him to the 10th century A. D.

I now proceed to deal with one who is deservedly famous as one of the greatest writers on Aesthetics *viz.*, Anandavardhana, the author of *Dhvanyaloka.* He belonged to the middle of the 9th century A. D. The work is divided into three parts—*viz.*, the *karikas* (brief statements), the *vritti* (the exposition) and the illustrations. The author of the Karikas seems to be different from the author of the vritti, if the view of Abhinavagupta, the author of *Lochana* (a commentary on the *Dhvanyaloka*), is correct. There is not, however, sufficient and satisfactory evidence for the view that *Sahridaya* was the author of the Karikas or that Anandavardhana was his pupil. The full name of Lochana is *Kavyalokalochana.* Abhinavagupta wrote also the *Abhinavabharati* which is a commentary on Bharata. He is equally famous as the auther of great philosophical works on Kashmir Shavaism. He belonged to the end of the 10th century.

Rajasekhara, who belonged to the 10th century A. D. and was the author of many poems and dramas, is the author of the valuable work on

Aesthetics known as *Kavya Mimamsa.* Mukula Bhatta's *Abhidha Vrittimatruka* belongs to the tenth century. Bhatta Tirtha's *Kavya kautuka* and Bhatta Nayaka's *Hridaya Darpana* have not yet been recovered and published. The former held that the *Santha Rasa* was the greatest of the Rasas as it led to *Moksha* (liberation). Dhananjaya's *Dasarupaka* which is a famous work belonging to the tenth century is the standard treatise on Indian dramaturgy.

Kuntaka's (he is called also as Kuntala) *Vakrokti jivita* is a great work on Aesthetics. Mr. S. K. De has brought out an excellent edition of it in the Calcutta Oriental Series. Kuntaka lived about the middle of the 10th century A. D. He held that *Vakrokti* (charming and figurative and unfamiliar expression) is the soul of poesy. He calls *Vakratva* also by another word viz., *Vaichitriya.*

Rajanaka Mahima Bhatta's *Vyaktiviveka,* Bhoja's *Saraswati Kantabharana,* and Kshemendra's *Auchitya Vichara charcha* and *Kavikanthabharana* belong to the eleventh century A. D. Mahima Bhatta attacked the concept of *dhvani* and held that the suggested sense is only an inference from the expressed meaning. He belonged to

Kashmir. King Bhoja's work is in the main a compilation. Kshemendra was a native of Kashmir and wrote many works. His aesthetic doctrine was that Auchitya (appropriateness) is the essence of Rasa.

We now come to one of the greatest of the rhetoricians of the world—Mammata. He was a native of Kashmir and belonged to the later portion of the 11th century A. D. His great work *Kavya Prakasa* is both a summation and a source.

Ruyyaka, the author of *Alankara-Sarvasva*, belonged to the middle of the 12th century A. D. He wrote also *Kavya Prakasa Sanketa* (which is a commentary on Mammata's work), *Alankara Manjari*, *Sahitya Mimamsa*, *Alankaranusarini* (a commentary on Mahima Bhatta's *Vyakti Viveka*) *Nataka Mimamsa*, *Sahridaya Mimamsa*, *Alankara Vartika* etc.

Hemachandra and Vagbhata are well-known Jain writers on Aesthetics. The former lived from 1088 A. D. to 1177 A. D. and wrote *Kavyanusasana* and *Alankarachudamani*. The latter wrote the work known as *Vaghbhatalamkara*. He also belonged to the 12th century. These works are compilations in the main. Amarachandra's *Kavita-*

rahasya and Devesvara's *Kavikalplata* belonged to the 13th century. They are not works of much merit. Bhanudatta's *Rasa-Tarangini* and *Rasa-manjari* belong to the 13th century. To the same time belongs *Ekavali* of Vidyadhara. The famous Mallinatha, who wrote commentaries on the poems of Kalidasa and Magha and Bharavi and Bhatti, wrote a commentary, called *Tarala*, on *Ekavali.* He belonged to the end of the 14th century.

To the 13th century belong two famous works on Aesthetics—Jayadeva's *Chandraloka* and Visvanatha's *Sahityadarpana*. *Chandraloka* consists of ten chapters. The famous Appaya Dikshitar's famous work *Kuvalayananda* is a commentary on the section on *Arthalamkara* in Chapter V of Chandraloka. He lived in the 16th century. There is a tradition in his village Adayapalm in the North Arcot District that he died in 1625 A. D. He wrote also *Chitra mimamsa* and *Vritti Vartika*. He discusses 124 figures of speech—which is the largest number discussed in any work on Poetics. Visvanatha's work discussed dramaturgy also in great detail. He wrote also *Kavyaprakasa darpana*, which is a commentary on Mammata's work.

Vagbhata's *Kavyanusasana* and its commentary *Alankara Tilaka* written by himself belong to the 14th century. Vidyanatha's *Prataparudrayosobhushana* belongs to the same era. All the examples in it were composed in honour of the Kakatiya King Prataparudra. The work is popular in our Presidency and is studied along with *Kuvalayananda* of Appaya Dikshita. Mallinatha's son Kumarasvamin wrote on it a commentary called *Ratnapana* in the 15th century.

The last great work on Aesthetics is Jagannatha's *Rasagangadhara*. He defines Kavya thus :

रमणीयार्थप्रतिपादकः शब्दः काव्यम् ।

(Poesy consists of words embodying a charming idea).

He attacked Appaya Dikshita's *Chitramimamsa* in his *Chitramimamsa Khandana*. Appaya Dikshita's descendant Nilakanta Dikshita defended *Chitramimamsa* in his *Chitramimamsadoshadhikkara*.

Later writers on poetics are Govinda the author of *Kavya Pradipa*; Saradatanaya, the author of *Bhava Prakasa* ; Singabhupala, the author of *Rasarnava sudhakara* ; Rupa Goswami, the author of *Nataka chandrika* and *Ujjvala Nilamani* ; Kavi Karnapura, the author of *Alamkara Kaustu-*

bha ; Kavichandra, the author of *Kavya chandrika*; Vallabha Bhatta, the author of *Alankara Kaumudi*, Kesava Misra, the author of *Alamkara Sekhara* ; and Rajachudamani Dikshita, the author of *Kavya Darpana*. Rajachudamani Dikshita belonged to the earlier half of the 17th century A. D. An excellent edition of this work was recently brought out by the well-known Sri Vani Vilas Press of Srirangam in 1926. The *Sahitya Sara* of Achyuta Raya is an excellent manual of Aesthetics and belongs to 1831 A. D.

Mr. P. V. Kane in his valuable edition of *Sahityadarpana* has given a list of 872 works on aesthetics. Many of these works are not now extant. I made a research in the Sarasvati Mahal, Tanjore, in respect of works on aesthetics available there. I found in it *Alamkara Ratnakara* (author unknown), *Alamkara Suryodaya* by Yajnesvara Dikshita *Kavikalpalatika* (author unknown), *Kavitavatara* (author unknown), *Sahitya Chudamani* of Lauhitya Bhatta Gopala (which is a commentary on Mammata's Kavya Prakasa), *Kavyasara sangraha* of Srinivasa, *Madhudhara* by Sudhindra yati, *Rasasarvaswa* of Bhimeswara bhatta, *Sabdarthachintamani* and *Sabdabhedanirupanam* by Ramachandra Dikshitar and Narayana Sastri, *Sahitya Chintamani* by Vira Narayana, *Sahitya Mimamsa* and *Sahityaratnakara*. I found in it also the following works on Indian Erotics:—*Smaradipika* by Rudra, *Sringaramanjari* by Sahaji Raja, *Sringarabhedapradipa* by Harihara, *Panchasayaka* and *Ratirahasyam*. Special mention may be made here of *Alamkara Raghava* by Yajnesvara Dikshita and *Alankara Tilaka* by Bhanudatta which exist in the Sarasvathimahal. The former work is so called because all the illustrative verses in it are in praise of Rama. He says:

सहृदयहृदयचमत्कारित्वाभावेन अलंकारत्वाभावात् ।

(Poetic beauty cannot exist if there is no enkindling of delight in the heart of a man of taste by its fascinating expression).

In the latter work there is an attempt to describe the various elements of poesy by comparing the same to the various elements of human personality:

अथ रसा आत्मानः तेषां शरीरं काव्यं तस्य यति रीति वृत्ति दोष तदभाव गुणालंकारा इन्द्रियाणि व्युत्पत्तयः शक्तयः प्राणाः अभ्यासो मनः ॥

In Kasi Lakshmana Kavi's work on Alamkara found in the Sarasvathimahal we find the following excel-

6

lent description of the nature of poesy :

काव्यलक्षणं तु विलक्षणचमत्कारजनकतावच्छेदकशालि-धीविषयार्थप्रबोधकशब्दत्वं । चमत्कारवैलक्षण्यं तु अनिर्वचनीयं सहृदयहृदयैकवेद्यं ॥

In conclusion I shall refer briefly to the work called *Dandi Alamkaram* in Tamil. This work is based on the Sanskrit work and is one of the many junction-points of Sanskrit and Tamil literatures. It deals with பொருளணி (Arthalamkara) and சொல்லணி (Sabdalamkara) *i.e.*, figures of speech and verbal felicities. But it contains no exposition of the soul of poesy—an aspect of the subject which is elaborately dealt with only in Sanskrit works on Aesthetics.

CHAPTER IV.

The Development Of Indian Aesthetical Doctrine.

The earliest work on Poetics is Bharata's *Natya-Sastra*. It is one of the earliest and greatest works on Indian Aesthetics and Indian Arts. It refers to four poetic figures (alamkaras), ten poetic excellences (gunas), ten defects (*doshas*) and thirty-six characteristics (*lakshanas*) of poetic composition. These *lakshanas* are really either *alamkaras* or *gunas*. He refers only to four poetic figures, viz., *upama* (similie) rupaka (metaphor), dipaka (illuminer), and *yamaka* (repetition of words or syllables which are similar in sound). He defines *gunas* as the negative of *doshas* whereas Vamana regards *gunas* as positive and *doshas* as the negative of *gunas*. Bharata does not elaborate the ideas of *riti* and *dhvani* which came to the forefront during later times. He however emphasises *rasa* as he does not keep poetics and dramaturgy apart but considers them both as inter-connected things and deals especially with the drama (rupaka). According to him *bhava* (an emotional state of mind) becomes *rasa* when it attains a state of permanence (*Sthayi bhava*) and is intensified by *Vibhavas* (major causes) and *anubhava* (minor causes) and *Vyabhichari-bhavas* (accessory facts). He says : *Vibhavanubhava Vyabhichari samyogad rasa nishpathih.* (The achievement of rasa is by the union of vibhavas and anubhavas and Vyabhicharibhavas. According to him the primary rasas are Sringara (Love), raudra (Fury), Vira (heroism), and *bhibhatsa* (disgust). The four derivative rasas are : hasya (the comic) arising from Sringara, Karuna (the pathetic) arising from Raudra, *adbhuta* (the marvellous) arising from *Vira*, and *bhayanaka* (the terrible) arising from bhibhatsa. The eight sthayi-bhavas or permanent aesthetic moods corresponding to the above eight *rasas* are *rathi* (love), *hasa* (mirth), *krodha* (anger) *utsaha* (courage), *bhaya* (fear), *Jugupsa* (aversion), *vismaya* (wonder), and *soka* (sorrow). Bharata refers also to thirty-three *Vyabhicharibhavas* and eight *sattvika bhavas* (involuntary external manifestations of internal feeling). Chapter 6, 7, 16, 18, 20 and 22 of Bharata's Natya Sastra are the most important portions of his work so far as aesthetics are concerned.

Bhamaha's *Kavyalamkara* is an exposition of poetics proper; and even here it aims rather at describing poetic decorations than at showing the soul of poetic feeling. He cares more about objective and external charms than about subjective and in ward sweetness. *Sabda* (word) and *artha* (sense) form the body of poesy and *alamkaras* (figures of speech) form its decorations. The analogy of body and soul is of frequent occurrence in Indian poetics, the critics differing as to what is the *soul* of poesy (*kavya atman*) as different from the body of poesy (*kavya-sarira*) : All the Indian writers on Aesthetics emphasise the importance of *Sahitya i.e.*, the alliance of sound and sense.

Bhamaha tells us that the purpose of poetry is *kirthi* (fame) for the poet and *prithi* (pleasure) for the reader. He, like other writers on aesthetics, emphasises the need for *Prathibha* (poetic inventiveness). He says that it is due to the power resulting from practice in previous births. Vamana defines it well as Janmantara gata samskara Visheshah (special power resulting from practise in antecedent births). It has been defined also as *prajna nava navollekha salini* (the power of ever-new creativeness). It has however to be perfected by study and practice (*Vyutpatti* and *abhyasa*). Thus a high standard was set for a poet. A similar, though not as high, set of qualifications was required in the case of a *sahridaya* or *rasika* (a man of taste). Bhamaha says that faultless and embellished (nirdosha and salamkara) sabdartha (sound and sense) is true poesy. He does not attach much importance to *riti* or *marga* (diction or style) which was lifted to a high place in poetics by Dandin. Nor does he attach importance to *gunas* which Dandin and others regard as the elements of *riti*. He emphasises *alamkara* or poetic embellishment and deals with alamkaras and doshas in great detail. He attaches much importance to *Vakrokthi* which may be described as a fascinating indirectness and obliqueness of speech. He does not attach importance to *swabhavokthi* (natural mode of expression) to which Dandin attaches much importance. His conception of *Vakrokthi* implies really only a heightened and striking and charming and fascinating turn of phrase and idea. In a similar way Dandin says that an *atisayokthi* all the poetic figures depend, because it is the heightened expression that gives charm to human speech and idea. These ideas merely imply that the poet lifts ordinary speech to a poetic level by a heightening of idea and expression.

Kuntala elaborated the idea of *Vakrokthi* in his *Vakrokthi jurta* but in the later development of Indian Aesthetic doctrine it has no prominent place at all.

In Bhamaha the concept of *Rasa* does not rise to the attitude to which it ascended later on. To him *rasavat* is a figure of speech. Similarly *Vyangyartha* or *dhvani* (secondary and suggested sense) is not according to him the life of poesy. It is, how-ever, implied in some of the *alamkaras* or figures of speech dealt with by him viz. Vyajasthuthi, aprasthutha-prasamsa paryayoktha and samasokthi. He thinks that the suggested sense is but an accessory to the expressed sense. His followers Udbhata and Pratiharendaraja develop his doctrines in a clear and sikllful manner. All of them and Rudrata do not attach any importance to *riti* or diction which they evidently regard as dealing with the external or verbal aspect of expression and as depending on the presence or absence of compounds. Rudrata's work is remarkable for its analysis of figures of speech, though his contribution to Aesthetics is not so noteworthy as his contribution to Rhetoric. He divides the *sabdalamkaras* into *vakrokthi*, *slesa* (paronomasia), *chitra* (metrical and verbal *tour-de-force*), *anuprasa* (alliteration), and *yamaka* (rhyme) and the arthalankaras into the broad generic groups of *vastava* (reality), *aupamya* (comparison) *atisaya* (exaggeration) and *slesha* commingling).

Dandin and Vamana lay down that the life of poesy is *riti* (diction) which itself means really the sumtotal of the *gunas* (excellences). Thus in their hands *alamkaras* became the hand-maids of *gunas*, just as still later both became the handmaids of *rasa* and yet later *dhvani* came to occupy the seat of supremacy. The number of poetic figures also rose from Bharata's four *arthalamkaras* to Appaya Dishitar's one hundred and twenty. The classification of the figures has been of a varied character. Dandin deals with thirty-five *alamkaras*. He divides them into *swabhavokthi* (natural expression) and Vakrokthi (fascinatingly indirect expression). Vamana bases them on *aupamya* (similarity). I have referred above to Rudrata's classification. Ruyyaka classifies them into the following groups. (1) *aupamya* (comparison); (2) *Virodha* (contrast); (3) *srinkhala* (interlinkedness); (4) *nyaya* (imaginative reason); (5) *gudhartha-prathithi* (subtle and suggestive sense); and *samkara* (commingling of figures of speech).

Dandin does not minimise the importance of decorative speech (Alamkara) but he emphasises more the *gunas* or excellences constituting *marga* (style), which is really the same as *riti* which is eulogised by Vamana as the soul of poetry. Such *marga* is either *vaidarbha* or *gauda*. In the former the ten *gunas* or literary excellences are harmonised, but they are not so harmonised in the latter. They are *slesha* (compactness), *prasada* (clearness), *samata* (smoothness), *madhurya* (sweetness), *sukumarata* (softness), *arthavyakti* (explicitness), *udaratva* (elevation), *ojas* (forcefulness), kanthi (brightness) and *samadhi* (metaphorical expression). Some of these are hardly distinguishable from Alamkaras. Dandin defines Alamkaras as *kavyasobhakarah Dharmah* (elements of beauty and brightness in poesy). He thinks that gunas or elements of style or diction are more important than alamkaras or elements of decoration. Among alamkaras he does not attach much value to verbal tricks like *yamaka*. He attaches much importance to Arthalamkaras (decorativeness of idea) and refers to thirty-five of such figures of speech. He mentions thirty-two divisions of *upama* (simile). Like Bhamaha he declares that *atisayokti* is essential in all figures of speech. He uses the term

Vakrokti as inclusive of all figures of speech other than *svabhavokti.* He is remarkable in that he exalts the latter over the former and is thus almost unique among Indian rhetoricians in that he prefers a natural and simple and direct and plain description to an artificial and ingenious and indirect and figurative description. He enumerates ten *doshas* or literary faults and blemishes. These are almost identical with Bhamaha's list.

Vamana carries Dandin's ideas further and declares that style or diction is the soul of poesy (*Ritir Atma Kavyasya*), while *Sabdartha* (word and sense) form its body. According to him *riti* depends on the *gunas* and on verbal arrangement. According to him *Vaidarbhi* riti combines all the ten gunas, *Gaudi* excels in *Ojas* and *Kanti*, (forcefulness and brightness) and *Panchali* is full of *madhurya* and *saukumarya* (sweetness and softness). In short *riti* is the resultant of the union of *gunas* or literary excellences. Vamana clearly defines the ten *sabda gunas* and the ten *artha gunas*, though he describes them by the same words. The fact is that some of the Alamkaras of the Alamkara School are hardly distinguishable from some of the gunas of the Riti School. Vamana emphasises the importance—

next to that of the *gunas*—of *alamkara* in the sense of beauty (*soundaryam alamkarah*), before he proceeds to enumerate the poetic figures. According to him *gunas* are the causes of poetic charm (*kavya sobhayah kartaro dharmah*) while *alamkaras* are the heighteners of such charm (*tad-atisayahetavah*). Thus his view is that *riti* based on gunas is the soul of poesy whereas *alamkaras* are the jewels decorating the body of poesy *i.e.*, *sabdartha* (word and sense). He treats of only thirty figures of speech. He describes only two *Sabdalamkaras* viz., *yamaka* (rhyme) and *anuprasa* (alliteration). According to him *upama* (simile) is the basis of all poetic figures. He calls these by the expressive term *upama-prapancha* (the world of simile). In later writers *riti* sank to a subordinate place, because they laid stress more upon emotion than upon form in poetry.

Till this stage we have not seen the sovereignty of the *rasa-concept*, though it was certainly not unknown. Bhamaha lays down in 1, 2, that a *mahakavya* should delineate all the *rasas*. Dandin also says so. But *rasa* is not regarded as the very soul of poesy. Nay, it was included by Bhamaha and Dandin only as one of the figures of speech (viz., rasavat). Dandin knew *rasa* and *bhava* but regarded them as elements of *alamkara*. Vamana defines *Kanti Guna* (brightness) as *dipta-rasatvam* (having glowing *rasa*). Udbhata refers to Bharata's eight *rasas* and adds to it another *rasa* namely *santa rasa*. But his disquisition about *rasa* is only on the footing of its being an element in the *alamkara* called *rasavat*. Rudrata adds to the abovesaid nine rasas a tenth viz., *preyas*. But in all these earlier writers we have no indication of their realisation of *rasa* as the innermost essence of poesy. They are more busy with the external aspects of style and trope than with the emotional and aesthetic content of poetry.

The later development of aesthetic doctrine was in the direction of *Rasa and Dhvani*. This was inevitable. In Indian Aesthetics as in Indian metaphysics the progression was towads the innermost core of being. It reached the doctrine of *Rasa* in the former and the doctrine of the Atman in the latter. The later history of Aesthetics in India is only the history of the exposition of the doctrine of Rasa and Dhvani and of the working out of the nature of aesthetic beauty from within outwards.

The writers on Aesthetics discuss with great subtlety the question whether rasa is an effect or a concomitant or an inference. I do not think that it will be of much interest now to go into these wire-drawn subtleties of logic, however much they were to the taste of scholastic mentality. Lollata says that the *vibhavas* are the efficient cause (*karaka hetu*) of the *rasa.* But Sankuka says that they are only the *Jnapaka hetu* (the logical cause). But the weakness in the former theory is that the actor who personates the hero does not experience the hero's feeling but merely simulates it. The weakness in the latter theory is that no one takes the actor to be the hero himself and that the actor's simulated feeling can neither cause the *rasa* on or bring into existence an inference of such *rasa*, because a non-existent thing cannot be inferred to exist. Another theory is that it is the universal feeling as expressed through the particular character that enkindles rasa through the rasa-enkindling property of the words in which the feeling is expressed. Abhinavagupta says that Rasa is *abhivyakta* (manifested) and not *karya* (caused) or *jnapya* (inferred). Whatever may be the logically right view on this matter, there is no doubt that aesthetic thought in India took a decisive turn in the direction of inward grace as different from mere outward decoration. The function of poetry is to produce a reflection of a great feeling and to induce in the hearer or the reader the relish of a permanent aesthetic mood kindled by an inner kinship with the universal aspect of the particular emotion which is described as felt by the hero in the poem.

To this concept of *Rasa* the *Dhvani* school gave an added grace by the concept of *Dhvani*. The real charm of poesy is the element of suggestion which enriches the *rasa* element. The aesthetic elements of *alamkara*, *guna*, *rasa* and *Dhvani* combine to make kinetic our potential *vasanas* (impressions) of beauty and emotional realisation, and the resultant energy of aesthetic enjoyment is the *Rasasvada* or rasa-enjoyment. Just as love of life and fear of death are latent in us as the result of innumerable births and lives and deaths, even so the emotional potency is latent in us as the result of emotional experiences in other births. What the charms of words and sense and feeling and suggestion achieve is to make patent the latent emotions, and this passage from potential emotion to kinetic emotion is felt by us as *Rasasvada* or relish of aesthetic feeling. Such relish of emotion is as real as the relish of food. It relates to the subtle region of the mind just as the *rasas* of eatable things relate to the gross realm of the palate. This pure aesthetic feeling is inherent in the mind and the joy of it has to be set free from impeding obstacles and to be kindled by accessory impulses. Thus *rasa* is not something injected from without but is a blossoming of what was in bud within, poesy merely performing the function of the warming and illuminating beam of the sun. Such aesthetic delight is different from the delight of the senses in which there is the element of selfishness of impulse and shortness of duration. It is more akin to spiritual bliss but it is less intense and less infinite and less immortal than the Ananda (bliss) of the Soul.

Thus *dhvani* is the *vyangya-artha* or the suggested sense. It is elaborated by the Dhvanikara (his name is unknown) and his expounder and commentator Anandavardhana who is one of the master-minds of Indian Poetics and Aesthetics. A word has not only its denotative (*abhidha*) sense but has also its indicative (lakshana) sense, and its suggested (vyanjana) sense. The Dhvani theorists declare that those poems are the best wherein the *vyangyartha* (the suggested sense) transcends the *vachyartha* (the expressed sense.) Anandavardhana combats the views of those who would either deny *vyanjana* or reduce it to a product of *vachya* or *lakshana.* He says that below the *dhvani kavya* is the gunibhuta vyangya kavya (wherein the suggested sense is subordinate to the expressed sense) while the lowest of all is the *chaitra kavya* in which there is no suggested sense at all but there is mere verbal prettiness or marshalling of unsuggestive tropes.

Anandavardhana divides the *Dhvani-kavya* into two types viz., *avivakshita vachya* in which the expressed sense is not meant and the suggested sense is all in all, and *vivakshitanyapara vachya* in which the expressed sense is meant but is only the doorway to the suggested sense. The latter type falls into two classes viz., the *asamlakshya krama* where the passage from the expressed to the suggested sense is unconscious and *samlakshya krama* wherein such passage is conscious and is perceived. Under the former category come *rasa* and *bhava*, whereas under the latter category come *vastu* (suggestiveness of subject) and *alamkara* (suggestiveness of figures). This is very sound and subtle aesthetic reasoning. All that the poet can do is to express the *vibhavas* and the *anubhavas* and the *vyabhicharibhavas* and leave the aesthetic mood to come into the reader's heart's horizon in its own self-created beauty. The universal element in the expressed emotion quickens the latent emotional tendency in the reader till the quickened emotional tendency blossoms as an emotional state or *vritti* in the surface of consciousness. The *vibhavas* etc., are the *vyanjakas* or the manifesting causes while the *rasa* is the *Vyangya* or suggested emotional and aesthetic mood rising like a wave on the ocean of the consciousness under the magical spell of the moon of poesy.

Thus according to Anandavardhana, the *dhvani kavya*, wherein the *Vyangya* or the suggested sense is supreme, is the finest type of poesy whereas the *gunibhuta Vyangya kavya* wherein the suggested sense is subordinate and merely heightens the expressed sense, is an inferior type of poesy. Thus the old *rasavat* which was a trope was distilled and sublimated into the subtler aesthetic concept of *rasa*, and the old concept of *rasa* was distilled and sublimated into the even subtler aesthetic concept of *dhvani*. The aesthetic mood (*rasa*) rose from an ornament of speech into the soul of speech, and the soul (rasa) was afterwards found to be ensouled by an Oversoul (Dhvani).

Dhvani may further be *Vastudhvani* or a suggested thought, or *alamkara-dhvani* or a suggested grace of expression, or *rasa-dhvani* or a suggested aesthetic and emotional mood. The last is the highest of all. The *gunas* and *alamkaras* are the *angas* and (limbs) of the suggested *rasa*. Thus the Dhvani theorists have appropriated the *rasa*-concept and have sought to explain it as the supremely vital element out of all the suggestive and suggested elements of poesy. The value of their theory is that while *rasa* was accorded a supreme place, the value of suggestiveness of subject-matter and imaginative grace of speech was not ignored but these elements were worked into the aesthetic mood though in due subordination. According to them fact and imagination are of value as feeders of emotion. The *dhvani* school says that *gunas* heighten *rasa* and *alamkaras* embellish *rasa*. The *gunas* are stated to be *madhurya* (sweetness), *ojas* (energy), and *prasada* (limpid clearness). *Madhurya* is suitable to evoke the *rasas* of *Sringara* (love), *karuna* (pathos) and *Santhi* (peace). *Ojas* rouses the *rasas* of *Vira* (heroism), *raudra* (fury), and *bhibhatsa* (disgust). *Prasada* is pervasive quality suitable to all *rasas*. Thus the expressed qualities and graces kindle the unexpressed and inexpressible sweetness of relished emotional states which result in aesthetic delight. Thus subject and style and splendour of figurative speech are cooperant towards the great end of Aesthetic Bliss. Only the true lover of Art can really enjoy the brocade of imaginative speech and the velvet skin of sweetness and strength and clarity of style and at the same time realise the invisible sweetness of the soul of *rasa* which is behind the outer veil of graceful speech and inner veil of lovely style and which alone gives value, nay even life and existence, to them.

The evolution of Aesthetics in India in later times subsequent to Anandavardhana need not detain us long. Just as he disentangled suggestion from the meshes of expression and made it supreme, even os the later writers disentangle *rasa dhvani* (suggested emotion) from other aspects of *dhvani* and place it on the highest pedestal. But their contribution of original ideas is but small. In fact till we come to the great figure in Indian aesthetics—Mammata—we have only a few refinements of Anandavardhana's great aesthetic idea. Among these writers it is necessary to mention only Kuntala and Mahima Bhatta, because Abhinavagupta's great commentary (Lochana) on Anandavardhana merely explains and elaborates the latter's ideas. Kuntala is known as the *Vakrokthi Jivitakara* as he affirms that *Vakrokthi* (charm of expression) is the soul of poetry. He thus takes us again to the externals of poesy and is thus a rebel against the *rasa* theory and the *dhvani* theory. But his *Vakrokthi* which he uses like a *Mantram* (incantation) emphasises really an inclusive idea which assimilates *rasa* and *dhvani* as well, just as the later single words like *chamatkara* or *auchitya* and *Ramaniyatha* do, though the fact is not acknowledged. *Vakrokthi* is only, imaginative and unfamiliar and striking and magical and charming felicity of expression. The word is not more expressive or clear than other words used by him such as *Vaichitriya* or (unusual charm), *Vaidagdhya Bhangi Bhanithi* (cleverness of expression), and *Vichithi* (poetic grace). He means the same idea as Browning expresses in his well-known verse: "Art may tell a truth obliquely." His refusal to recognise *Swabhavokthi* (natural description) as poetry shows how his theory errs by over-statement. He however administered a needed corrective to the *rasa* theorists and *dhvani* theorists who attached too much importance to emotional mood and aesthetic suggestiveness and minimised the value of verbal felicity and adornment of speech. *Vakrokthi* is vague enough to include *rasa* and *dhvani* and is as impalpable in its texture as the rainbow itself. Just as the aestheticians who emphasised *alamkara* made *rasa* a subordinate element by including *rasavat* as a poetic figure and just as the *rasa* and *dhvani* theorists gave a place to *alamkara* similar to that of the porter at the gate. Kuntala brings up a new word i.e., *vakrokthi* and tries to make everything subservient to it. Mahima Bhatta's attempt to show that what is *vyangya* (suggested sense) is only an inference from the expressed sense is a clever logical *tour deforce* but his work is of little value as a contribution to our stock of aesthetic ideas.

Mammata is one of the greatest of Indian writers on rhetoric and aesthetics. He gives a due place in his system to *sabda and artha* (sound and sense), guna (merit), *dosha* (defect), *alamkara* (figure of speech), and also to *Vyanjana* or *dhvani* (suggestiveness) and *rasa*. He adopts Anandavardhana's threefold classification of poetry into *dhvani*, *gunibhutavyangya* and *chitra*. According to him *gunas* are factors intensifying *rasa*, and *alamkaras* are only jewels adorning *Sabdartha* which form the body of poesy. Such adornment is primarily to the body but as the body is of value only as the temple of the soul, the adornment is finally only to the soul of poesy which is *Rasa*. Even without *alamkaras* there could be true poetry, but the charm of poetry is heightened by them.

Another great work is Viswanatha's *Sahitya-Darpana*. He says that *rasa* is the soul of poesy. (*Vakyam rasatmakam kavyam*). But there is no substantial difference between his view and the views of Anandavardhana and Mammata. According to him there are only three *gunas* viz., *madhurya*, *ojas* and *prasada*. He values them and *riti* only as feeders of *rasa*. He values *alamkaras* only as secondary and mediate adornments leading to the intensification of *rasa*. Neither his work which is an excellent manual on poetics nor Ruyyaka's *Alamkara Sarwaswa* contains any strikingly original aesthetic ideas. Vidyadharas's *Ekavali* and Vidyanatha's *Prataparudriya* are only clear and clever compilations. In the latter work *sabda and artha* (sound and sense) are described as the body of poesy, *gunas* as the qualities (like the qualities of men such as heroism etc.,) *alamkaras* as the ornaments, and *Vyangya* as the soul. He describes also *Sayya* or interlinked and harmonious repose of expression and *paka* or ripeness of utterance. The portion of his work which deals with drama elaborately is based on Dhananjaya's *Dasarupaka.* Hemachandra's *Kavyanusasana,* like the earlier Bhoja's *Saraswathi Kantabharana,* belongs to the group of compilations. Kesava Misra's *Alamkara Sekhara* and Achuta Raya's *Sahitya-Sara* and Visweswara's *Alamkara Kaustubha* are also similar valuable compilations. Jayadeva's Chandraloka and Appaya Dixita's Kuvalayananda which is a commentary on it are valuable manuals and are very popular in South India.

In Jagannatha's *Rasagangadhara,* which is not available in a complete form we find great ingenuity and subtlety but not much of originality. He is a relentless critic of Appaya Dixita. He defines *Kavya* as *ramaniyartha pratipadakah sabdha* or a composition expressing a charming idea. This charm induces an unselfish and pure and disinterested and impersonal delight. This *ramaniyatha* or *chamatkara* is a vague word and leads us nowhere just like *Ishtartha* of *Dandin* and *Vakrokthi* of Kuntala or other terms like *hridyatva, charutva, Auchitya, soundarya, vichitri,* or *vaichitrya.* This capacity to enjoy aesthetic loveliness is what is called taste and it is partly natural (i.e., inherited from previous births) and partly formed by continued search for and enjoy-of the beautiful in the realm of reality and in the realm of ideas. A sense-delight is selfish and personal but in aesthetic delight which can be enjoyed by all there is an impersonal and disinterested character (*alaukika* or *lokottara*) which lifts it near spiritual delight. That is the reason why even fear and grief which are disliked in personal contact are relished in impersonal contact. The word which expresses this pure aesthetic delight is *rasa*. Jagannatha gives primacy to *dhvani* and divides poesy into four grades according to the descending supremacy of *dhvani* in it (*uttamottama, uttama, madhyama, adhama*). He regards *gunas* as heightness of *rasa* and accepts, like Mammata, only three gunas viz. Madhurya, Ojas and Prasada causing three mental states viz., *druthi* (melting tenderness), *dipti* (brilliance), and *vikasa* (blossoming). He then discusses rhetoric proper and deals with about seventy poetic figures. He says that the source of feeling and expression is the inventive and soaring imaginative reason of the poet (*kavi-prathibha*) which is partly due to *vasana*, partly to tradition (*sampradaya*) and partly to imaginative intention (*anubhava*.)

There was no strikingly great work on Indian Æsthetics after Jagannatha's *Rasagangadhara.* Rudrabhatta's *Sringaratilaka*, Bhoja's *Sringara-prakasa*, Saradatanaya's *Bhavaprakasa*, and Singa-Bhupala's *Rasarnavasudhakara* are excellent manuals and nothing more. In Kshemendra's *Auchityavichara* he says that *auchitya* (propriety) is the life of *rasa* and is based on *chamatkara* or charm of expression. His *Kavi Kantabharana* describes how an unpoetical person may become poetical, how the gifted poet can attain great gifts, what are the faults to avoid and the excellences to attain in poetry, and what general culture will increase the beauty of the poet's imaginative expression. Rajasekhara's *Kavya mimamsa* is of some value. It describes the pedigree of poesy and says that *Kaya Purusha* was the son of Sarasvati and married *Sahityavidya vadhu.* He describes *sahitya* as the union of sound and sense (शब्दार्थयोर्यथावत्सहभावेन विद्या साहित्यविद्या). He shows the importance of the various factors in poetic composition *viz., sakti* (genius), *pratibha* (imaginative intention), *Vyutpatti* (culture), and *abhyasa* (practice).

If I may venture to suggest a principle of co-ordination of views on these vital points of aesthetics, I may say that rasa is the soul of the goddess of Art; *vyangya* or *dhavani* is her life; *gunas* are her mental qualities; *Sabdartha* is her body; arthalamkaras are her natural ornaments just as brilliance of complexion, beauty of tresses, beauty of forehead and eyes, dimpled chin, rose-red bloom of lips, lissom figure, and charm of gait are natural graces to womanhood; and *Sabdalamkaras* are her beauty of dress and decoration. Any attempt to exalt any one of the elements at the expense or to the exclusion of the others cannot but stultify itself. The above analysis is but a many-sided and multiple presentation of a unity, as the personality of the goddess of poesy is a divine unity in a divine variety. Some rhetoricians say that the gunas abide in poetry by *Samavaya Vritti* whereas the alamkaras abide in it by *samyoga vritti.* Stripping these terms of their logical subtleties, the above view would affirm that guna is an inseparable and ever-present element whereas alamkara is a separable element and need not be and may not be always present. It seems to me that *arthalamkaras* also are as indispensable and inseparable as *gunas* and that sabdalamkaras—wisely used not for their own sake but for the sake of adding new graces—are really equally indispensable though theoretically separable. The exclusive pursuit of *Rasa* and *Dhvani* sometimes leads to that straining after the unexpresssed which, as time passes and as poets exhaust the stock of emotions, results in the mere hunt after conceits and remote effects, just as the pursuit of *Vakrokti* leads to entire loss of touch with directness of utterance and the reality of things. Aesthetic emotion and aesthetic expression should be in touch with reality and sincerity and directness and then add the gleams of beauty which bring an added sweetness to the emotion and an added grace to the expression. Such added sweetness and grace may now come from verbal felicity and felicity of style or even from the mere sounds of letters or mere felicities of alliteration and assonance and rhyme. They will come more often from beautiful figures of speech which, by the power of expression of comparisons and contrasts and identifications and affinities and superiorities, will bring out new aspects of loveliness in the idea. They will come still more often by the realisation and expression of the sweet intricacies and endearments of human emotions with their primary and subsidiary manifestations. The element of suggestiveness, like the secondary rainbow, will bring that elfin music and elusive sweetness which are the sweetest things in life. All these may or may not combine. But the highest art is to conceal art. Any perceived straining after this or that effect will spoil our relish altogether. If a mind revelling in beauty and dowered with imagination allows its overflow of bliss to course in this or that channel of verbal felicity or decorative speech or emotional expression or subtle suggestive sweetness in a natural manner according to surge of the aesthetic mood, there will result that combination of art and artlessness, that combination of "natural magic" and "moral profundity" (to use the famous words of Matthew Arnold), which is the acme of poetic expression. The special danger which will wreck the artistic expression of those who are too much under the influence of this or that theory about "the soul of poesy" is that they will carry the theory of decorativeness or emotionalism or suggestiveness too far. I am afraid that it is this defect that has spoiled to some extent Indian Nature Poetry and Indian Poetry about God. In the Upanishads the Poetry about God is grand and sublime and natural but in later poetry about God there is a little too much of the intrusion of aesthetic theories into the region of the overflow of spiritual ecstacy into human speech. Examples of Indian poetry expressive of the elevating influence of natural phenomena —the vast spaces of earth, the glories of vegetation, the mighty mountains, the perennially stupendous sea, the clouds lit with lightnings and rainbows, the blue depths of space, the wheeling glories of the heavens, the celestial distances that dwarf and humble the human imagination, the faint and tenuous glories and luminosities which are worlds in the making—are but few. If technical *rasa* or *dhvani* must come in here, it will be an unwelcome intruder and nothing more. We have to keep apart the *rasa* of human emotions and the *rasa* of Nature and the *rasa* of God. *Rasa* is no doubt the soul of Art. But there are not merely many forms of *rasa* but many grades and types of *Rasa*. We have to galvanise and electrify Indian æsthetics and Indian Art in such a way that we can preserve the perfections already attained and add new perfections from our study of the Art and Aesthetics of the West so that Art may again be in our land "a priest to us all of the wonder and bloom of the world" and Aestheties may again be in our land a priest to us all of the wonder and bloom of Art.

CHAPTER V.

The Aesthetic Concept of Rasa.

Thus the fundamental aesthetic concept completed its cycle and began with *rasa* in Bharata and ended with *rasa* in Anandavardhana and Mammata and later writers. Its life-history is like the life-history of the soul itself *viz.*, from Ananda (bliss) through diversity to Ananda again. It is like the evolution of sound from the *shadja* sound in the lower key to the *shadja* sound in the higher key.

Rasa is the soul of poesy. The only refinement introduced by Anandavardhana is that *rasa* itself belongs to the region of *suggestion* (*dhvani*). This merely expresses one of the elements of *rasa* and does not bring in any concpt in supercession or modification of the concept of *rasa*. *Rasa* (aesthetic pleasure) is kindled in the reader or hearer by the poet and the playwright. The aesthetic mood is unlike the delight of the senses. The latter is selfish and direct and personal. The former is unselfish and indirect and impersonal. The latter cannot be tasted in commonalty but the former can. That is why

Wordsworth refers to "Joy in widest commonalty spread". In the ideal world even pain and grief are robbed of their sting and kindle aesthetic pleasure. This delight is akin to aesthetic spiritual delight. But in the former there is the element of mentality while in the latter we have only pure spirit which transcends mind and matter alike. It, like *Atmananda*, is *Svasamvedya* (self-realised) and *lokottara* (world-transcending) and *niyatikrita-niyamarahita* (free from the fetters of destiny, and *hladaikamaya* (of the essence of joy) and *ananya-paratantra* (self-poised and not dependent on something external) and *nirmiti* (creativeness).

The Indian analysis of the aesthetic concept of *Rasa* is as acute and perfect as the Indian analysis of the metaphysical concept of the *Atman*. The following well-known verse of Bharata cannot be quoted and discussed too often.

विभावैरनुभावैश्च सात्विकैर्व्यभिचारिभिः ।
आनीयमानः स्वाद्यत्वं स्थायीभावोरसः स्मृतः ॥

He says also विभावानुभावव्यभिचारिसंयोगाद्रसनिष्पत्तिः।
The dominating emotion (the *ruling passion*, to use Pope's words) is described by the word *sthayibhava*.

It is thus defined :

सजातीयविजातीयैरतिरस्कृतमूर्तिमान् ।
यावद्रसं वर्तमानः स्थायीभाव उदाहृतः ।

It blossoms into *rasa* (a relishable and joy-enkindling pervasive aesthetic mood) when it is heightened and intensified by विभावाः *Vibhavas* (the principal exciting and stimulating causes *i.e., Alambanavibhavas* as well as the aceessory stimulating causes *i.e., uddipanavibhavas*), अनुभावाः *anubhavas* (external manifestations such as sidelong glances, smiles etc)., *sattvikabhavas* (prominent physical effects) *Vyabhicharibhavas* (ever-changing and ever-rising and ever-setting minor *collateral* feelings of pleasure and pain). Thus the Vibhavaś are causes which bring into manifestation the mind-imbedded *vasanas* of *sthayibhavas*, such *vasanas* having come to us as a karmic endowment from past births. *Alambanavibhavas* are the human *factors* in emotion and *Uddipanavibhavas* are the environmental factors in emotion.

The above elements of *rasa* are dealt with in great detail and with great subtlety and minuteness by Indian writers on æsthetics. Rasa is kindled by *Vibhavas* manifested by *anubhavas* and intensifed by *Vyabhicharibhavas.* I can do no more than indicate the main features here. *Vibhava* means that which supports and nourishes the main sentiment, *Alambana vibhava* is the chief basis of the rasa. It refers to the hero or the heroine. *Uddipana vibhavas* are the factors intensifying the rasa. They are the moon, the south wind, the *Kokila* (the cuckoo) etc.. in the case of the love emotion (*sringara rasa*). *Anubhava* has been thus defined :

अनुभावो विकारस्तु भावसंसूचनात्मकः ।

Thus Anubhavas are such physical factors as the beloved's glance etc., which bring the *sthayibhavas* into the plane of the working consciousness. *Sattvika Bhavas* are certain prominent physical effects of feeling. Bhava is the pervasion of the mind by a predominant feeling. Kalidasa brings out its relation to Rasa in the 5th canto of the *Kumarasambhava* where Uma refers to her love of Siva thus :—

ममात्र भावैकरसं मनः स्थिरं न कामवृत्तिर्वचनीयमीक्षते ॥

(My mind is full of an intense mood of longing. Love does not heed scorn).

Sattvika refers to that mental attitude which identifies us with the joys and sorrows of others.

परमतदुःखहर्षादिभावनायामत्यन्तानुकूलान्तःकरणत्वम् ॥

(Having a mind which is very prone to identify itself with griefs and joys of others).

Thus Sattvika Bhavas are a specially important group out of the general group of *Anubhavas.*

पृथग्भावा भवन्त्यन्ये तेऽनुभावत्वेऽपि सात्त्विकाः ।
सत्वादेव समुत्पत्तेस्तच्च तद्भावभावने ॥

"एतदेवास्य सत्वं यतः खिन्नेन प्रहर्षितेन चाश्रुरोमाञ्चादयो निर्वर्त्यन्ते तेन सत्त्वेन निर्वृताः सात्त्विकाः ॥"

The *Sattvika Bhavas* are the following :

'स्तम्भप्रलयरोमाञ्चाः स्वेदो वैवर्ण्यवेपथू ।
अश्रुवैस्वर्यमित्यष्टौ'

(Passivity, loss of consciousness, horripilation, sweating, loss of brightness, tremor, tears, and change of tone).

Vyabhicharibhavas are the waves on the ocean of the *sthayibhavas.*

विशेषादाभिमुख्येन चरन्तो व्यभिचारिणः ।
स्थायिन्युन्मग्ननिर्मग्नाः कल्लोला इव वारिधौ ॥

They are thirty-three in number *viz.*, satiety, langour, apprehensiveness, weariness, mental repose, deadness of faculties, exultation, depression sternness, anxiety, fear, jealousy, anger, arrogance, memory, collapse, vanity, dream, sleep, wakefulness, bashfulness, possesion by evil spirits, stupor, prudence, indolence, agitation, ratiocination, dissimulation, mental pain, delirium, despair impatience and indecision.

त्रासेर्ष्यामर्षगर्वाः स्मृतिमरणमदाः सुप्तनिद्राववोधाः
व्रीडापस्मारमोहाः समतिरलसतावेगतर्कावहित्था ।
व्याध्युन्मादौ विषादोत्सुकचपलयुतास्त्रिंशदेते त्रयश्च ॥

It has been further said.

विरुद्धैरविरुद्धैर्वा भावैर्विच्छिद्यते न यः ।
आत्मभावं नयत्यन्यान्स स्थायी लवणाकरः ॥

Thus the *sthayibhava* (permanent æsthetic mood) blends the various accessory moods (unless they are thoroughly contrary to it) into a greater and intenser totality. Thus even *bibhatsa* (disgust) is pressed into the service of Sringara (love) in Malati-Madhava. This is what is called *Angangibhava* (inter-relation of secondary and primary entities).

Thus *rasa* is a complex æsthetic phenomenon. It is a subjective æsthetic mood kindled in the reader or the hearer or the seer by his sharing in the depicted feelings because of the universal elements present in such delineation Such unselfish absorption in an æsthetic mood enables the innate bliss of the soul to shine forth There is then a breaking of the prison-bars of innate delight (आवरणभङ्ग) This joy is described by Indian æstheticians in almost as rapturous terms those in which as the *Ananda* (Bliss) of the *Atman* is described by the Indian metaphysicians

I have referred already to Mammata's descriptions of poetic creativeness and poetic bliss in his famous work *Kavyaprakasa*

Visvanatha says in his *Kavyadarpana*

सत्त्वोद्रेकादखण्डस्वप्रकाशानन्दचिन्मयः ।
वेद्यान्तरस्पर्शशून्यो ब्रह्मास्वादसहोदरः ॥
लोकोत्तरचमत्कारप्राणः कैश्चित्प्रमातृभिः ।
स्वाकारवदभिन्नत्वेनायमास्वाद्यते रसः ॥

(Rasa—which, arising from the exaltation of the *sattvaguna*, is infinite and full of self-luminous bliss and consciousness, which is free from the taint of any other intruding mental act, which is akin to the experience of Divine Bliss, whose soul is transcendent charm,—is enjoyed by some happy and fortunate experiencers and enjoyers as a unity of enjoyer and enjoyed and enjoyment)

It has been said by almost all the writers on Indian Aesthetics that the *Sthayibhavas* are eight *viz.*, रति, हास, शोक, क्रोध, उत्साह, भय, जुगुप्सा, and विस्मय, and that these give rise to the eight rasas (*Sringara, hasya, karuna, raudra, vira, bhayanaka, bibhatsa* and *Adbhuta—i.e.*, Love, the comic, pathos, fury, heroism, terror, disgust, and the marvellous). The presiding deities are said to be Vishnu, Pramatha, Yama, Rudra, Indra, Kala, Mahakala and Brahma. There are four Vrittis or styles of composition. *Kaisiki Vritti* is said to be appropriate for the delineation of *Sringara*, *Sattwati* is appropriate to *Vira rasa*, *Arabhati* is appropriate to *raudra rasa*. *Bharati Vritti* is common to all the *rasas*. *Udbhata* includes *Santi* (peace) as the ninth *rasa*. Its presiding deity is stated by Visvanatha to be Narayana. Rudrata mentions a tenth rasa *viz.*, *preyas* (friendship). Visvanatha mentions *Vatsalya* (love for the young) as the tenth rasa. Those who concede *santirasa* say that *nirveda* (dispassion) is its *sthayibhava*. Some however declare that it cannot be represented in a drama, because the purpose of a drama is to kindle and not to stifle passion.

Bhoja thinks that *sringara* (love) is the sole *rasa* which gives rise to the other rasas as its modifications. Visvanatha quotes with approval *Narayana's* dictum that *Adbhutarasa* is the basic *rasa*.

रसे सारश्चमत्कारः सर्वत्रानुभूयते ।
तच्चमत्कारसारत्वे सर्वत्राप्यद्भुतो रसः ।
तस्मादद्भुतमेवाह कृती नारायणो रसम् ॥

It is further stated that the four main mental states are विकास (blossoming), विस्तार (expansion), क्षोभ (agitation), and विक्षेप (unsettlement) and that they lead to the four sentiments *viz.*, *Sringara*, *Vira*, *Bibatsa* and *raudra* which in their turn lead to *hasya*, *adbhuta*, *bhayanaka* and *karuna* (including *santi*) respectively.

The fact is that all these theories have in them a great deal of fanciful speculation. Even the view about eight rasas, though it has the support of great and many authorities, is not absolutely correct. The figure eight can be regarded only as illustrative and not as exhaustive. *Rasa* is only a primary emotion or sentiment. It is no doubt true that love, mirth, pity, ambition, anger, fear, horror and wonder are such primary emotions. But the circle of primary emotions is not filled only with these sentiments. Even in the past the theory was widened by extending *Rati* to love of God and of holy men and by extending heroism (*Vira*) beyond heroism in battle (*yuddha vira*) so as to include *dharma vira* and *dana vira* and *daya vira i.e.*, heroism of virtue, and the heroism of munificence, and the heroism of compassion (*e.g.*, in Nagananda), as also *satya vira* (heroism of truth) *vidya vira* (heroism of knowledge), *tapo vira* (heroism of austerity), *yoga vira* (heroism of *yoga*), *kshamavira* (heroism of forgiveness), *ahimsa vira* (heroism of non-injury) *etc.*, I showed above how *preyas* and *Vatsalya* were brought in. The supreme *rasa* of Bhukti has come in whether orthodox æsthetics will recognise it or not. In Rupa Gosvami's *Ujjvala Nilamani madhurya rasa* which is the highest form of *bhakti* (higher than *santi*, and *dasya* or *priti*, and *sakhya* or *preyas*, and *Vatsalya*) is described as the supreme rasa (*ujjvala rasa*). For this *rasa*, he describes *krishna rati* (the love of Krishna) as the *sthayi-bhava*. The *bhakta* (the devotee) takes the place of the *sahridaya* (the man of taste). In modern times patriotism (love of country) and humanitarianism (love of humanity) must be received into the magic circle of the *rasas*. In short, Indian æsthetics was a growing art and should not refuse grow hereafter.

Thus though the writers on æsthetics mention only eight *rasas* and grudgingly add Santhi as the ninth rasa, it cannot be doubted that Bhakti should be elevated to the rank of a *rasa* nay to the rank of the supreme rasa. Its *Alambana Vibhava* is God the Eternal Beauty and the Eternal Beloved; its *uddipana Vibhava* is the sum total of His *Vibhuthis*; its *anubhavas* are tears of joy etc; its *Vyabhichari-bhavas* are supreme delight etc. The Bhakti rasa fills the mind with rapture which not even Sringara Rasa can rival. It is different from Santi because Prema is of a different category from Vairagya. It has been well said in *Bhagavad Bhakti Chandrikamritarasollasa* :

परत्रानासङ्गं जनयति रतिर्या नियमतः
परास्मिन्नेवास्मिन् समरसतया पश्यत इमम् ।
परप्रेमाढ्येयं भवति परमानन्दमधुरा
परा भक्तिः प्रोक्ता रस इति रसास्वादनचणैः ॥

(Supreme devotion, which unfailingly creates an indifference to other and lower things, which is realised as inseparable from the Supreme, which has the affluence of the highest affection, and which is sweet with the most exquisite bliss has been accepted as a *rasa* by the expert enjoyers of *rasas*.)

CHAPTER VI.

The Fundamental Concepts of Indian Rhetoric.

THE word most frequently employed to express Rhetoric is *Alamkara Sastra*. I have discussed above the doctrines of the various schools of poetics in the order of date *viz.*, the *rasa* school, the *alamkara* school, the *riti* school, the *dhvani* school, the *Vakrokti* school, and the *auchitya* school. They stressed emotion, figures of speech, style, suggestiveness, a fascinating uncommonness of idea and expression, and propriety of idea and expression. I proceed to deal now with a few general concepts peculiar to poetics and not common to all branches of Aesthetics. It will not be possible to deal here with each individual figure of speech and its illustrations. But a few general concepts of Indian Rhetoric are well worth discussion and elaboration here.

One very valuable idea in Indian poetics is about poetic temperament and poetic equipment.

11

It emphasises the fact that there are three important factors *viz.*, *Pratibha* (inventive and intuitive imagination), *Vyutpatti* (culture), and *abhyasa* (practice). Of these factors the most important is *pratibha* because it is by its aid that the poet sees visions of beauty and gives them sweet and picturesque and melodious expression. The poet is "a priest to us all of the wonder and bloom of the world." A famous definition of *Pratibha* is: प्रज्ञा नवनवोन्मेषशालिनी प्रतिभा मता (It is the mental gift which enables one to realise ever-new aspects of beauty and give them ever-new radiances and harmonies of expression). Thus the Indian conception includes the three vital elements of artistic creation *viz.*, Vision, creativeness, and form. A well-known passage describes with great acuteness how the poetic imagination realises the beauty of things in moods of perceptive joy and meditative rapture and then blossoms into perfect expression.

रसानुगुणशब्दार्थचिन्तास्तिमिततेजसः ।
क्षणं विशेषस्पर्शोत्था प्रज्ञैव प्रतिभा कवेः ॥

स हि चक्षुर्भगवतस्तृतीयमिति गीयते ।
येन साक्षात्करोत्येष भावांस्त्रैलोक्यवर्तिनः ॥

Another fine idea in the works on Poetics is that Poesy is the fulfiller of the aims of life (Purusharthas) including the highest aim of life *i.e.*, Moksha. Visvanatha says in his *Sahityadarpana.*

चतुर्वर्गफलप्राप्तिः सुखादल्पधियामपि ।
काव्यात्......

(From poesy the attainment of the four Purusharthas will come easily to persons of even limited mental power).

It has been said well by Bhamaha :

धर्मार्थकाममोक्षेषु वैचक्षण्यं कलासु च ।
करोति कीर्तिं प्रीतिं च साधुकाव्यनिषेवणम् ॥

Kuntaka carries the idea a step further and says :

चतुर्वर्गफलास्वादमप्यतिक्रम्य तद्विदाम् ।
काव्यामृतरसेनान्तश्चमत्कारो वितन्यते ॥

(By the enjoyment of the nectar of poesy is created a bliss which transcends the realisation of even the four Purusharthas).

Kavyas have been divided into *Padya* (those in pure verse), *gadya* (those in pure prose), and *misra* (those in mixed verse and prose). I have already referred to the division into the very best, उत्तमोत्तम), the best (उत्तम), the moderately good

(मध्यम) and the lowest (अधम). I have referred also to Ananda Vardhana's division into ध्वनिकाव्य and गुणीभूतव्यङ्ग्यकाव्य and चित्रकाव्य. Dramas are described as Drisya (seen) kavyas while poems are श्रव्य (heard) kavyas. There are also elaborate rules as to what topics should be described if a Kavya is to be called महाकाव्य. It should not be less than 8 cantos or more than 30 cantos in length.

चतुर्वर्गफलोपेतं चतुरोदात्तनायकम् ।
नगरार्णवशैलर्तुचन्द्रार्कोदयवर्णनैः ॥
उद्यानसलिलक्रीडामधुपानरतोत्सवैः ।
विप्रलम्भैर्विवाहैश्च कुमारोदयवर्णनैः ॥
मन्त्रद्यूतप्रयाणाजिनायकाभ्युदयैरपि ।
अलंकृतमसंक्षिप्तं रसभावनिरन्तरम् ।
काव्यं कल्पान्तरस्थायि जीयेत सदलंकृति ॥(Dandin)

One of the excellences of Indian rhetoric lies in its clear and close and cogent analysis of the power of the word and of the varied significance of speech. There is a vital difference between the expressed sense (वाच्यार्थ) and the figurative sense (लक्ष्यार्थ). In the well-known instance गङ्गायां घोषः the *lakshya* meaning is "a hamlet on (the bank of) the Ganga," though the *vachya* meaning is "a hamlet on the Ganga." The implication (व्यङ्ग्य) is that it will have the Gangetic qualities of coolness and holiness. To use the technical language of Sanskrit Aesthetics, the प्रयोजन (purpose) of a लक्षणा (secondary and figurative sense) is व्यङ्ग्य (suggestiveness). In some instances the joy resulting from suggestion may not be localisable in any specific word but is real all the same.

The grammarians laid down that each sound leaves a स्फोट (sphota) which may be called a reflex or impression. Very probably the *Dhvani* theory had its origin therein. Just as the uttered word (sabda) merely gives an embodiment to the disembodied sound (sphota), even so the *Sabdartha* of the writers on aesthetics is said to be the व्यञ्जक (the manifesting cause) of the व्यङ्ग्य or the inner sense to which the outer or Vachya sense is subordinate. Hence *rasa* is not *created* so much as *manifested.* This again is in accord with the Vedantic theory of creation. Hence the delectation in the heart of the poet or the dramatist can kindle a kindred mood only in a man of taste (सहृदय or रसिक).

Such being the possibilities of power in words, the Indian rhetoricians teach us how to use words in such a way as to bring out all the potentialities in them so that words may be powerful allies in the creation of aesthetic delight. The first important element is faultlessness. Hence the rhetoricians study carefully the possible *doshas* (faults). Then we must aim at auspicious qualities (gunas). These are compared to courage and other qualities of a man. We must then add the jewelled graces of *alamkaras* (figures of speech). These are compared to the jewels worn by human beings. But all these must subserve the supreme end and aim of all poesy *viz.*, Rasa. Bhoja sums up these ideas in his well-known verse:

निर्दोषं गुणवत्काव्यमलंकारैरलंकृतम् ।
रसात्मकं कविः कुर्वन्कीर्तिं प्रीतिं च विन्दति ॥

(The poet, composing poems free from faults and full of good qualities and decorated with figures of speech and endowed with *rasa* as soul, attains fame and delight.)

The question of *Doshas* (demerits) is as important as that of *gunas*. Bhoja divides them into पददोष, वाक्यदोष and वाक्यार्थदोष (Padadosha, Vakyadosha, and Vakyarthadosha). The *Pada doshas* (verbal infelicities) are:

असाधु चाप्रयुक्तं च कष्टं चानर्थकं च यत् ।
अन्यार्थकमपुष्टार्थमसमर्थं तथैव च ॥

अप्रतीतमथ क्लिष्टं गूढं नेयार्थमेव च ।
सन्दिग्धं चाविरुद्धं च प्रोक्तं यच्चाप्रयोजकम् ।
देश्यं ग्राम्यमिति स्पष्टा दोषाः स्युः पदसंश्रयाः ॥

A detailed explanation of these will swell this volume into one of tremendous proportions. I may say that these defects are such as vitiate the beauty of the words : *e.g.*, words which are ungrammatical, words which are unused by poets, unharmonious words, mere expletives, unusual use of words, circumlocutous words, purposeless words, slang words, obscene words etc. The *Vakya Doshas* (infelicities of sentence-construction) are:

शब्दहीनं क्रमभ्रष्टं विसन्धिपुनरुक्तिमत् ।
व्याकीर्णं वाक्यसंकीर्णं अपदं वाक्यगर्भितम् ॥

द्वे भिन्नलिङ्गवचने द्वे च न्यूनाधिकोपमे ।
भग्नच्छन्दो यती च द्वे अशरीरमरीतिमत् ॥

These are repetition, erroneous epithet, errors of metre, grammatical lapses, etc. The *Vakyartha doshas* are :

अपार्थं व्यर्थमेकार्थं ससंशयमपक्रमम् ।
खिन्नं चैवातिमात्रं च परुषं विरसं तथा ॥

हीनोपमं भवेच्चान्यदधिकोपममेव च ।
असदृशोपमं चान्यदप्रसिद्धोपमं तथा ।
निरलंकारमश्लीलं विरुद्धमिति षोडश ॥

We may characterise these as infelicities of meaning such as meaninglessness, absence of significant purport, dubious expression, roughness of expression, lack of charm in expression, lapse from propriety in figurative expression, divergence from Dharmasastra and Arthasastra and Kamasastra, etc.

The insistence on the avoidance of *doshas* (demerits) is surpassed by the emphasis on the indispensableness of *gunas* (merits). Bhoja says in his *Sarasvati Kanthabharana*:

अलंकृतमपि श्राव्यं न काव्यं गुणवर्जितम् ।
गुणयोगस्तयोर्मुख्यो गुणालंकारयोगयोः ॥

He enumerates the gunas thus :

श्लेषः प्रसादः समता माधुर्यं सुकुमारता ।
अर्थव्यक्तिस्तथा कान्तिरुदारत्वमुदात्तता ॥

ओजस्तथान्यदौर्जित्यं प्रेयानथ सुशब्दता ।
तद्वत्समाधिः सौक्ष्म्यं च गाम्भीर्यमथ विस्तरः ॥

संक्षेपः संमितत्वं च भाविकत्वं गतिस्तथा ।
रीतिरुक्तस्तथा प्रौढिरथैषां लक्ष्यलक्षणे ॥

These are such qualities of style as a beautiful combination of words, clarity, an equable level of style, sweet simplicity, mellifluousness, splendour of utterance, stateliness of sound, interlinkedness of words, interweaving of liquid sounds, sweet and subtle expression, description of animation in inanimate objects, suggestiveness, fulness, brevity, dignity etc.

The basic classification of Alamkaras has differed from time to time. The classification into शब्दगत (relating to words), अर्थगत (relating to sense) and उभयगत (relating to both) was simple but not subtle. It was elaborated in Agni Purana and Bhoja's *Sarasvati Kanthabharna*. Later on an attempt was made to base the differentiation on similarity, identity and contrast. *Prataparudriya* states that the principles of classification are as follow :

साधर्म्य {
अभेदप्रधान—*e. g.*, रूपक, अपह्नुति.
भेदप्रधान—*e. g.*, दीपक, तुल्ययोगिता, निदर्शन, सहोक्ति, प्रतीप, व्यतिरेक.
भेदाभेदसाधारण—*e. g.*, Upama.
}

अध्यवसाय—*e. g.*, Utpreksha, Atisayokti.

विरोध—*e. g.*, Vibhavana, Viseshokti ;

वाक्यन्याय—*e. g.*, Parisamkhya etc.

लोकव्यवहार—*e. g.*, Svabhavokti, Vinokti, etc.

तर्कन्याय—*e. g.*, Kavyalinga, Anumana, Arthantara-nyasa.

शृंखलावैचित्र्य—*e. g.*, Karanamala, Ekavali, Maladipaka.

अपह्नव—*e. g.*, व्याजोक्ति, वक्रोक्ति.

विशेषणवैचित्र्य—समासोक्ति, परिकर.

But such attempts are artificial and have always been more or less failures. It was and is and will be always difficult to thrust in all the alamkaras into one or other of such compartments. The subtle Indian intellect went on discovering new Alamkaras and each such discovery left the previous classifications in the lumber of rejected principles of classification.

Bhoja describes the twentyfour *Sabdalamkaras* thus:

जातिर्गती रीतिवृत्तिच्छायामुद्रोक्तियुक्तयः ।
भणितिर्गुफना शय्या पठितिर्यमकानि च ॥
श्लेषानुप्रासचित्राणि वाकोवाक्यं प्रहेलिका ।
गूढप्रश्नोत्तराध्येयश्रव्यप्रेक्ष्याभिनीतयः ॥

Jati refers to the group of languages *e.g.*, Sanskrit, Prakrit, Vernaculars etc. Gati refers to prose, poetry and prose-poetry. *Reeti* refers to the vaidarbhi, Panchali, Goudi, Avantika, Lati and Magadhi styles. It refers to the style being simple or ornate. Bhoja describes them thus :

तत्रासमासा निःशेषश्लेषादिगुणगुंफिनी ।
विपञ्ची स्वरसौभाग्या वैदर्भी रीतिरिष्यते ॥

समस्तपञ्चषपदामोजःकान्तिविवर्जिताम् ।
मधुरां सुकुमारां च पाञ्चालीं कवयो विदुः ॥

समस्तात्युद्भटपदामोजः कान्तिगुणान्विताम् ।
गौडीयेति विजानन्ति रीतिं रीतिविचक्षणाः ॥

अन्तराले तु पाञ्चाली वैदर्भ्योर्यावतिष्ठते ।
सावन्तिका समस्तैः स्याद्द्वित्रैस्त्रिचतुरैः पदैः ॥

समस्तरीतिव्यामिश्रा लाटीया रीतिरुच्यते ।
पूर्वरीतेरनिर्वाहे खण्डरीतिस्तु मागधी ॥

I do not think that these subtle distinctions among the Vaidarbhi, Panchali and other styles is of any real value. Equally devoid of real significance is the classification into kaisiki, arabhati, bharati, satvati, madhymarabhati, and madhyamakaisiki *vrittis*. These correspond to the mental states of equilibrium and pleasure, exalted dignity and might, an intermediate state between softness and sternness etc. Bhoja defines them thus:

सुकुमारार्थसंदर्भा कैशिकी तासु कथ्यते ।
या तु प्रौढार्थसंदर्भा वृत्तिरारभटीति सा ॥

कोमलप्रौढसन्दर्भा कोमलार्था स भारती ।
प्रौढार्था कोमलप्रौढसंदर्भा सात्त्वतीं विदुः ॥

कोमले प्रौढसंदर्भा त्वर्थे मध्यमकैशिकी ।
प्रौढार्था कोमले बन्धे मध्यमारभटीष्यते ॥

Chhaya is using the current speech. That there is a beauty in using it aptly is thus described by Ratnesvara: लोके बिंबप्रतिबिंबयोः प्रतिबिंबं चमत्कारितया प्रसिद्धम् । Mudra is suggestiveness of expression. The other words do not deserve any minute discussion here. *Sayya* corresponds to style. *Yamaka* is a similarity of words containing a diversity of import. Rhyme is but one aspect of such similarity. Bhoja defines *yamaka* thus:

विभिन्नार्थैकरूपाया या वृत्तिर्वर्णसंहतेः ।
अव्यपेतव्यपेतात्मा यमकं तन्निगद्यते ॥

An extreme illustration is

समानयासमानया स मानया समानया ।
समानया समानया समानया समानया ॥

Slesha has been thus defined :

एकरूपेण वाक्येन द्वयोर्भणनमर्थयोः ।
तन्त्रेण यत्सशब्दज्ञैः श्लेष इत्यभिशब्दितः ॥

In it different words have the same sound *e.g.*,

तस्याविनापि हारेण निसर्गादेव हारिणौ ॥

Anuprasa has been thus defined :

आवृत्तिर्या तु वर्णानां नातिदूरान्तरस्थिता ।
अलंकारः स विद्वाद्भिरनुप्रासः प्रदर्श्यते ॥

Bhoja praises it thus :

यथा ज्योत्स्ना चन्द्रमसं यथा लावण्यमङ्गनाम् ।
अनुप्रासस्तथा काव्यमलंकर्तुमयं क्षमः ॥

अनुप्रासः कविगिरां पदवर्णमयोऽपि सः ।
सोऽप्यनेन स्तबकितः श्रियं कामपि पुष्यति ॥

It is the recurrence of the same letter in different words in such a way as to heighten the resonant splendour of the verse. But Bhoja overrates it too much.

उपमादिविमुक्तापि राजते काव्यपद्धतिः ।
यद्यनुप्रासलेशोऽपि हन्त तत्र निवेश्यते ॥

कुण्डलादिविमुक्तापि कान्ता किमपि शोभते ।
कुङ्कुमेनाङ्गरागश्चेत्सर्वाङ्गीणः प्रयुज्यते ॥

The following is a ridiculous instance of it :

ननो ननुन्नो नुन्नेनो नानानाना ननाननु ।
नुन्नोऽनुन्नो ननुन्नेनो नानेनानुन्ननुन्नन् ॥

Here is another such instance in Tamil :

வானகக்தரு மிசைய வாயின
வானகக்தரு மிசைய வாயின
வானகக்தரு மிசைய வாயின
வானகக்தரு மிசைய வாயின.

It is not possible to discuss the subtleties of discussion in Indian aesthetics about figures of speech. I shall refer here to a few major Arthalamkaras (figures of speech) by way of sample out of the one hundred and forty and odd tropes discussed in the books on Poetics. The essence of *Upama* (simile) is similitude. Johnson said well that a perfect simile "must illustrate and ennoble the subject". I give here a few of its many definitions.

यत्किंचित्काव्यबन्धेषु सादृश्येनोपमीयते ।
उपमा नाम सा ज्ञेया गुणा कृतिसमाश्रया ॥

(Bharata's Natya Sastra).

यच्चेतोहारिसाधर्म्यमुपमानोपमेययोः ।
मिथो विभिन्नकालादिशब्दयोरुपमा तु तत् ॥

(Udbhata's Kavyalamkara Samgraha).

उपमानेन उपमेयस्य गुणलेशतः साम्यमुपमा ॥

(Vamanas' Kavyalamkara Sutra).

उपमानोपमेययोः साधर्म्ये भेदाभेदतुल्यत्वे उपमा ।

(Ruyyaka).

साधर्म्यमुपमा भेदे ।

(Mammata).

चमत्कारिसाम्यमुपमा ।

(Vagbhata's Kavyanusasana).

हृद्यं साधर्म्यमुपमा ।

(Hemachandra's Kavyanusasana).

उपमानोपमेयत्वयोग्ययोरर्थयोर्द्वयोः ।
हृद्यं साधर्म्यमुपमेत्युच्यते काव्यवेदिभिः ॥

(Appayya Dikshita's Chitra Mimamsa).

सादृश्यं सुन्दरं वाक्यार्थोपस्कारकमुपमालंकृतिः ।

(Jagannatha's Rasagangadhara).

It has been well said about *upama* that it is the mother of alamkaras and that it illumines the universe:

अलंकारशिरोरत्नं सर्वस्वं काव्यसंपदाम् ।

उपमा कविवंशस्य मातेवेति मतिर्मम ॥

तदिदं चित्रं विश्वं ब्रह्मज्ञानादिनोपमाज्ञानात् ।
ज्ञातं भवतीत्यादौ निरूप्यते निखिलभेदसहिता सा ॥

Appayya Dikshita says in his *Chitra Mimamsa* :

उपमैकाशैलूषी संप्राप्ता चित्रभूमिकाभेदान् ।
रञ्जयति काव्यरङ्गे नृत्यन्ती तद्विदां चेतः ॥

In fact *upama* by a little change becomes one or another of other figures of speech. If we say that "your face is like the moon" it is *upama* (चन्द्र इव मुखं). If we say that "the moon is like your face" it is प्रतीप (मुखमिव चन्द्रः). If we say "your face is the moon", then we have रूपक (मुखमेव चन्द्रः). If we say "this is the moon and not a human face", it is अपह्नवः (चन्द्रोऽयं न मुखं). If we say "your spotless face is superior to the spotted moon" it is व्यतिरेकः (निष्कलंकं मुखं चन्द्रादतिरिच्यते).

Dandi defines Rupaka (metaphor) as तिरोभूतभेदा उपमा (a simile in which the similitude is hidden). Bharata had defined it thus :

स्वविकल्पैर्विरचितं तुल्यावयवलक्षणम् ।
किंचित्सादृश्यसंपन्नं यद्रूपं रूपकं तु तत् ॥

Bhamaha says :

उपमानेन यत्तत्त्वमुपमेयस्य रूप्यते ।
गुणानां समतां दृष्ट्वा रूपकं नाम तद्विदुः ॥

Vamana says :

उपमानेनोपमेयस्य गुणसाम्यात तत्त्वारोपो रूपकम् ।

Thus metaphor is simile condensed into identity. There is in it a superimposition (आरोप) of the उपमान (the illustration) on the उपमेय (the object). In fact in it the object of description and the object of comparison are fused into a bright and incandescent unity.

Dipaka (illumination) has been so called because like a lamp on a terrace it illumines both the terrace and the road. Dandi defines it thus :

जातिक्रिया गुणद्रव्यवाचिनैकत्रवर्तिना ।
सर्ववाक्योपकारश्चेत् तदाहुर्दीपकं यथा ॥

Udbhata says :

आदिमध्यान्तविषयाः प्राधान्ये नरयोगिनः ।
अन्तर्गतोपमाधर्माः तत्र तद्दीपकं विदुः ॥

Vamana says :

उपमानोपमेयवाक्येष्वेका क्रिया ।

Mammata says :

सकृद्वृत्तिस्तु धर्मस्य प्रकृताप्रकृतात्मनाम् ।

Jagannatha says :

प्रकृतानामप्रकृतानां चैकसाधारणधर्मान्वयो दीपकम् ।

In *Vyatireka* (contrast) the elements of contrast and similitude mingle but the vital element in the figure is its superstructure of contrast based on the substratum of similarity. Dandi says :

शब्दोपात्ते प्रतीते वा सादृश्ये वस्तुनोर्द्वयोः ।
तत्र यद्भेदकथनं व्यतिरेकः स कथ्यते ॥

Jagannatha says :

एवं च प्रतीयमानमपि सादृश्यं गुणान्तरकृतनिषेधो-स्थापिते न उत्कर्षेण हतप्रभमिव बन्दीकृतमिव न चमत्कार-विशेषमभिधातुं प्रभवतीति प्राचामाशयः ।

Rudrata says :

यो गुण उपमेये स्यात् तत्प्रतिपन्थी च दोष उपमाने ।
व्यस्तसमस्तन्यस्तौ तौ व्यतिरेकं त्रिधा कुरुतः ॥

Another important figure of speech is *atisayokti* (hyperbole). The true hyperbole is as inevitable an expression of man's infinite aspiration as the Gothic spire or the *gopuram* (tower) of an Indian temple. Dandi finely describes it thus :

विवक्षाया विशेषस्य लोकसीमातिवर्तिनी ।

असावतिशयोक्तिः स्यादलंकारोत्तमा यथा ॥

Bhamaha and Udbhata says :

निमित्ततो वचो यत्तु लोकातिक्रान्तगोचरम् ।
मन्यन्तेऽतिशयोक्तिं तामलंकारतया यथा ॥

Hemachandra says :

विशेषविवक्षया भेदाभेदयोगायोगव्यत्ययोऽतिशयोक्तिः ॥

Vagbhata says :

अत्युक्तिरतिशयोक्तिः ॥

Vamana says :

संभाव्यधर्मतदुत्कर्षकल्पनाऽतिशयोक्तिः ।

Bhoja says :

सा च प्रायो गुणानां च क्रियाणां चोपकल्प्यते ।
न हि द्रव्यस्य जातेर्वा भवत्यतिशयः क्वचित् ॥

प्रभावातिशयो यश्च यश्चानुभवनात्मकः ।
अन्योन्यातिशयो यश्च तेऽपि नातिशयात्पृथक् ॥

अलंकारान्तराणामप्येकमाहुः परायणम् ।
वागीशमहितामुक्तिमिमामतिशयाह्वयाम् ॥

About *Utprekhsha* (Poetic Fancy) it has been well said :

उत्प्रेक्षा हरति स्वान्तं अचिरोढास्मितादिव ।

Dandi defines it thus :

अन्यथैव स्थिता वृत्तिश्चेतनस्येतरस्य वा ।
अन्यथा प्रेक्ष्यते यत्र तामुत्प्रेक्षां विदुर्यथा ॥

Udbhata says :

साम्यरूपविवक्षायां वाच्येवाद्यात्मभिः पदैः ।
अतद्गुणक्रियायोगादुत्प्रेक्षातिशयान्विता ॥

Bhamaha says :

अविवक्षितसामान्या किंचिच्चोपमया सह ।
अतद्गुणक्रियायोगादुत्प्रेक्षातिशयान्विता ॥

Vamana says :

अतद्रूपस्यान्यथाध्यवसानमातिशयार्थमुत्प्रेक्षा ।

Vagbhata says :

अत्यन्तसादृश्यादसतोऽपि धर्मस्य कल्पनमुत्प्रेक्षा ।

Bhoja says :

अन्यथावस्थितं वस्तु यस्यामुत्प्रेक्ष्यतेऽन्यथा ।
द्रव्यं गुणः क्रिया चापि तामुत्प्रेक्षां प्रचक्षते ॥

Mammata says :

संभावनमथोत्प्रेक्षा प्रकृतस्य समेन यत् ।

While उपमा (simile) is an imaginative effort to link two like things in one act of poetic consciousness, Utpreksha aims at a brief and delightful suggestion of similarity as realised from a new and original angle of inner vision.

Svabhavokti (natural description) is not unknown in Sanskrit poetry as some traducers of our poesy affirm. Dandi defines it thus :

नानावस्थं पदार्थानां रूपं साक्षाद्विवृण्वती ।
स्वभावोक्तिश्च जातिश्चेत्याद्या सालंकृतिर्यथा ॥

It is called also स्वभाव, स्वरूप and वास्तव. Rudrata says :

वास्तवमिति तज्ज्ञेयं क्रियते वस्तुस्वरूपकथनं यत् ।
पुष्टार्थमविपरीतं निरुपममनतिशयमश्लेषम् ॥

It is not mere description of the thing as it is that constitutes *Svabhavokti.* The description should be a strikingly beautiful description. The Sahitya Darpana says : स्वभावोक्तिर्दुरूहार्थ स्वक्रिया रूपवर्णनम् । A comic instance of a charmless natural description is the following :

दीर्घपुच्छश्चतुष्पादः ककुद्मांल्लंबकंबलः ।
गोरपत्यं बलीवर्दस्तृणमत्ति मुखेन सः ॥

This recalls Johnson's instance :

I put my hat upon my head and walked into the Strand ;

And there I met a man whose hat was in his hand."

The following are charming instances :

तुण्डैराताम्रकुटिलैः पक्षैर्हरितकोमलैः ।
त्रिवर्णराजिभिः कण्ठैरेते मञ्जुगिरः शुकाः ॥

कलक्वणितगर्भेण कण्ठेनाघूर्णितेक्षणः ।
पारावतः परिक्षिप्य रिरंसुश्चुम्बति प्रियाम् ॥

आक्रोशन्नाह्वयन्नन्यानाधावन्मण्डलैरुदन् ।
गावारयति दण्डेन डिम्भः सस्यावतारिणीः ॥

Sanskrit æsthetics has not worked out all the beauties of Svabhavokti as it deserves. It was lured away by subtler and more glittering blossoms of speech. In Sanskrit Poetry less attention was bestowed on it than on them. Dandi however says about it:

शास्त्रेष्वस्यैव साम्राज्यं काव्येष्वप्येतदीप्सितम् ।

Vakrokti has been used in different senses. It has been defined by Dandi and others as an ornamental way of description as opposed to a matter-of-fact description (स्वभावोक्ति). From this point of view every figure of speech will come under it. The *Srutanupalini* says :

स्वभावोक्तिर्नाम यथावस्थितपदार्थरूपकथनं वक्रोक्ति-

र्नाम यथावस्थितमन्यथीकृत्य । अत्र उपमादयः संकीर्णप-र्यन्ताः वक्रोक्तिषु पतिताः स्वभावोक्तिः पुनराद्यालंकारः ।

Kuntaka, who is known as the वक्रोक्तिजीवितकार went so far as to say that Vakrokti is the life of poesy. Mahima Bhatta explains that view thus in his Vyakti Viveka :

शास्त्रप्रसिद्धशब्दार्थोपनिबन्धनव्यतिरेकि यद्वैचित्र्यं त-न्मात्रलक्षणं वक्रत्वं नाम काव्यस्य जीवितमिति सहृदयमा-निनः केचिदाचक्षते ।

Bhamaha regards Vakrokti as an element of Alamkara. वक्राभिधेयशब्दोक्तिरिष्टा वाचामलंकृतिः । Using it in a loose sense, it has been brought near Ati-sayokti.

Mammata says :

सर्वत्र विषयेऽतिशयोक्तिरेव प्राणत्वेनावतिष्ठते । तां विना प्रायेणालंकारत्वायोगात् ।

Abhinavagupta says :

यातिशयोक्तिर्लक्षिता सैव सर्वा वक्रोक्तिः अलंकारप्र-कारः सर्वः । लोकोत्तरेण चैवातिशयः । तेनातिशयोक्तिः सर्वालंकारसामान्यम् ।

Vamana's view of Vakrokti as based on सादृश्य

(सादृश्यालक्षणा वक्रोक्तिः ।) is a more restricted view. According to him उपमा is the basic figure, whereas the earlier school regarded vakrokti or atisayokti as the basic figure. Ruyyaka and others restrict its scope further. Ruyyaka says :

अन्यथोक्तस्य वाक्यस्य काकुश्लेषाभ्यामन्यथा योजनम् ।

Some even call it a Sabdalamkara based on *slesha*. We may say that in general it is a clever and original turn of sentiment and expression. (वैदग्ध्यभङ्गी भणितिः)

It has been well said :

प्रसिद्धं मार्गमुत्सृज्य यत्र वैचित्र्यसिद्धये ।
अन्यथैवोच्यते सार्थः सा वक्रोक्तिरुदाहृता ॥

Slesha (paronomasia) is a means of heightening the poetic charm and effect in every figure of speech. Dandi says :

श्लेषः सर्वासु पुष्णाति प्रायो वक्रोक्तिषु श्रियम् ।
भिन्नं द्विधा स्वभावोक्तिर्वक्रोक्तिश्चेति वाङ्मये ॥

The commingling of specific alamkaras is itself a source of beauty. Some even regard it as a separate *alamkara* by itself. Bhamaha says :

वरा विभूषा संसृष्टिर्बह्वलंकारयोगतः ।
रचिता रत्नमालेव सा चैव मुदिता यथा ॥

Vamana says :

अलंकारस्यालंकारयोनित्वं संसृष्टिः । तद्भेदावुपमारूपकोत्प्रेक्षावयवौ ॥

Ruyyaka says :

तत्र यथा बाह्यालंकाराणां सौवर्णमणिमयप्रभृतीनां पृथक्चारुत्वहेतुत्वेऽपि संघटनाकृतचारुत्वान्तरं जायते तद्वत् प्रकृतालंकाराणामपि संयोजने चारुत्वान्तरं उपलक्ष्यते । तेन अलंकारान्तरप्रादुर्भावो न पृथक्पर्यवसानमिति निर्णयः ॥

Bhoja says in his Sarasvatikanthabharana :

जायते न च दोषाय काव्येऽलंकारसंकरः ।
विभूषयति हारोऽपि स्तनौ ग्रीवां मृगीदृशाम् ॥

I must desist from pursuing this interesting study further. Indian Rhetoric is by itself a complicated subject which has been dealt with in a subtle and fascinating way. I desire here only to indicate its fundamental concepts and its general aspects and leave the reader to turn with delight to one of the most fascinating branches of Indian literature and Indian æsthetics.

CHAPTER VII.

The Fundamental Concepts of Indian Dramaturgy.

INDIAN drama is acknowledged on all hands to be a great literary achievement in the literature of the world. In India, as elsewhere, the origin of the drama was humble. It began as an adjunct to religious ceremonial. Puranic stories and recitations and dramatised versions of the Puranas afforded religious instruction and refined amusement during leisure hours on the occasion of Sattra-yagas. Drama originated in pantomime and then added to itself the dialogue and the lyrical element. The Indian drama differs from the Greek drama, in form and content. In the Greek drama the unities of time and place and action are observed; there is a severe simplicity of outline; and there is no passionate search for the Infinite. But in Indian drama, as in the modern romantic drama, the unities of time and place are ignored, the unity of action alone being observed; there is a profusion of adornment of fancy and imagination ; and there is a linking up of the finite with the Infinite. The one great deficiency in Indian drama is the absence of tragedies. Historical plays are but few and are not fired by the spirit of intense patriotism such as the history and destiny of the country amply demand and justify. In course of time the Indian classical drama became overweighted with rules and conventions and pandit-riddden and lifeless and wooden and bereft of popular appeal. The popular plays went merrily along as an artistic amalgam of empty song and coarse buffoonery. The amateur stage in modern India is trying to link up the two and to infuse fresh blood from the west. But its successes hitherto have been but slight. Tagore has broken new ground but he has achieved greater success as a poet rather than as a playwright. My aim, however, in this work is not to deal with Indian dramaturgy and so I resist the temptation to deal with Indian dramas in detail, and especially the plays of Kalidasa, the greatest dramatist of India.

The Indian rhetoricians differentiate between *Natya*, *Rupa*, and *Rupaka*, *i.e.*, representation of emotions, presentation of individual situations, and a regular drama.

अवस्थानुकृतिर्नाट्यं रूपं दृश्यतयोच्यते ।

रूपकं तत्समावेशाद्दशधैव रसाश्रयम् ॥

(Dhananjaya's Dasarupaka)

The differentiation deals with the three aspects rather than with the three categories. *Natya* refers to the aspect of the identification of the actor with the character ; *Rupa* refers to the aspect of appeal to the sight ; and *rupaka* refers to the development of the aspects of identification and visibility into the presentation of the imaginative world of the play.

The ten *rupakas* or forms of drama are Nataka, Prakarana, Bhana, Prahasana, Dima, Vyayoga, Samavakara, Veethi, Anka, and Ihamriga. These are elaborately described in Dhananjaya's *Dasarupaka*, Visvanatha's *Sahityadarpana*, and Vidyanatha's *Prataparudriya*. If they are to be discussed here this chapter alone will swell to the size of a book. I may however say a few general words about *Nataka* which is the norm of which the others are only variants. In it the *sutradhara* or conductor enters and pronounces the benedictory stanza (नान्दी श्लोक). Then follows a prologue (प्रस्तावना) in which we have some description of the author and the work, some singing and some indication of the character about to enter. The hero should be a *Dhirodatta* (heroic and noble and well-known man). There should be a prevailing *rasa* (æsthetic mood) which would be well developed by the elements of *rasa* described already in an earlier chapter. The main *rasa* should be *Shringara* (love) or *Vira* (heroism), the other rasas introduced being congruous and contributory to the main *rasas*. A Nataka should have five acts. Seven acts also are allowed. A Mahanataka may have ten acts. Battles, coarse love-making, kissing, etc., should not be exhibited on the stage. The play should close with a prayer (भरतवाक्य).

Among the other *rupakas* may be specially mentioned *Prakarana* and *Prahasana*. In *Prakarana* the plot should be a fiction based on real life. *Prahasana* is a farce. The *Uparupakas* are subsidiary dramatic forms. They are natika, trotaka, goshti, sattaka, natya, rasaka, prasthana, ullapya, kavya, prenkhana, rasaka, samlapaka, srigadita silpaka, vilasika, durmallika, prakarani, halleesa, and bhanika. In *Natika*, the hero should be a king of the *dhiralalita* type (described below) and love should be the chief sentiment. The Trotaka should contain 5, 7, 8 or 9 Acts. Both celestial and human characters should be introduced. The *Vidushaka* should be present in each Act and love should be the prevailing sentiment.

Every play should have *Vastu* (plot), *Neta* (hero) and *Rasa* (sentiment). The main plot is called *Adhikarika vastu.* The minor or subsidiary plot is continuous (पताका) or discontinuous and occasional (प्रकरि). In a play devoted to Rama, the minor plot about Sugriva would be a *Pataka* while the incident about Jatayu or Sabari would be a Prakari. The Vastu (plot) may be historical (प्रख्यात) or invented (उत्पाद्य) or composite (मिश्र).

As the rhetoricians fixed their gaze on the development of *rasa* (emotion) as the main element in a drama, they resorted to various devices to recapitulate briefly intermediate events. *Vishkambha* shows the connection between past and future events by the dialogue of some characters other than the chief characters. *Pravesaka* is a dialogue between low characters indicating future events. *Choolika* is the hinting of incidents by characters behind the scenes. *Ankasya* is the showing of the connection between two Acts by the speech of characters at the end of an Act. *Ankavatara* is that wherein the germ of the next Act is given at the end of the preceding Act. All these fulfil the function of the *Chorus* in the dramas of Greece.

The rhetoricians refer also to *Sarvasravya or prakasa* which is a dialogue to be heard by all ; to *asravya* or *svagata* which means soliloquy, to *Janantika* which means what one says to another to the exclusion of others, to *apavarita* which means turning back to whisper a secret to another, and to *Akasabhashita* where one on the stage pretends to hear something said by one who is not on the stage and to repeat it.

The means by which the plot is carried on from its commencement to its conclusion are called *Bija, Bindu, Pataka, Prakari* and *Karya.* I have referred to *Pataka* and *Prakari* above. *Bija* is the germ of the story. *Bindu* is what patches any breaks in the story. *Karya* is attainment and has the following stages or *Avasthas viz.,* *Arambha* or hopeful beginning, *yatna* or endeavour, *praptyasa* or hope of attainment, *niyatapti* or certainty of attainment and *Phalayoga* or attainment. The rhetoricians refer also to five *sandhis i.e., Mukha* where the seed of the *rasa* is sown, *Pratimukha* where we have the sprouting of the seed, *Garbha* where we have in turn the realisation and the non-realisation of the end desired, *Avamarsa* where there is a certainty of attainment, and *Nirvahana* or attainment.

Indian æsthetics deals with the various classes of lovers. It divides them into *anukula* (faithful), *dakshina* (attached to many), *satha* (शठ *i.e.*, roguish) and *dhrishta* (bold and saucy). The hero is grouped also as *Dhirodatta* (brave and high-spirited and noble), *dhriodhata* (brave and proud), *dhiralalita* (brave and sportive), and *dhiraprasanta* (brave and serene). Each one of these may be *anukula* or *dakshina* or *satha* or *dhrishta*. Besides describing the types of heroes, books describe also the *pitha-marda* (the comrade of the hero), *vita* (the dependent of the hero), and *vidushaka* (the juster or buffoon. The rival hero is called Pratinayaka, *e.g.* Ravana in opposition to Rama and Duryodhana in opposition to Yudhishthira.

The theorists state further that the hero should have eight special excellences *viz.*, *sobha* (brilliance, cleverness etc), *vilasa* (vivacity), *madhurya* (sweetness), *gambhirya* (profound self-possession), *sthairya* (steadfastness), *tejas* (prowess and keen sense of honour), *lalitya* (gracefulness and sportiveness) and *audarya* (munificence).

Similarly the heroine is classified as *sviya* (wife), *parakiya* (another's wife), or *samanya* (courtesan). The *sviya* is classified as *mugdha* (young and artless), *madhya* (youthful), and *pragalbha* (mature and masterful). Each of these is again grouped as *dhira* (self-possessed), and *adhira* (weak and tearful). The *parakiya* may be a maid or a married woman. The Indian æstheticians clearly lay down that she should never be the chief heroine. The main *rasa* should not be pourtrayed with reference to her. The writers on Indian Poetics lay down also that the *samanya* (courtesan) should not be introduced into a play except in a farce (*Prahasana*) and that if she is brought in she should be delineated, like Vasantasena in Mrichchakatika, as being devoted to one lover alone. Professor Wilson has said well: "We may observe, however, to the honour of the Hindu drama, that the *parakiya* or she who is the wife of another person, is never to be made the object of dramatic intrigue; a prohibition that would have sadly cooled the imagination, and curbed the wit, of Dryden and Congreve".

The Sanskrit rhetoricians group heroines further into *svadhinapatika* (whose husband is obedient and devoted to her), *Vasakasajja* (dressed and decorated and expectant of her lover), *utka* or *virahotkanthita* (disappointed in her assignation) *vipralabdha* (deceived), *kalahantarita* (seperated owing to a quarrel), *khandita* (angry at sight of her lover's unfaithfulness), *abhisarika* (going to meet her lover), and *proshitapatika* (pining for her absent lord).

The characteirsties of youthful women are elaborately delineated. They are grouped into three physical embellishments *viz.*, *bhava* or first rise of emotion and *hava* or movement of eyes and brows indicating the awakening of feeling and *hela* or the clear manifestation of emotion; seven natural and inherent qualities *viz.*, radiance of youth, brilliance of beauty, brightness due to passion, sweetness, self-possession, munificnce and courage, and ten natural graces *viz.*, sportiveness, charming manifestation of feeling, fascination of careless decoration, tremor, hysterical combination of anger and tears and joy, involuntary expression of affection, bashful denial and repulse of amorousness, affected indifference to endearments, amorous and graceful gait and gesture, and bashful nability to avow passion.

यौवने सत्वजाः स्त्रीणामलंकारास्तु विंशतिः ।
भावो हावश्च लीला च त्रयस्तत्र शरीरजाः ॥

शोभा कान्तिश्च दीप्तिश्च माधुर्यं च प्रगल्भता ।
औदार्यं धैर्यमित्येते सप्तभावा अयत्नजाः ॥

लीलाविलासो विच्छित्तिर्विभ्रमः किलकिंचितम् ।
मोट्टायितं कुट्टमितं बिब्बोको ललितं तथा ।
विहृतं चेति विज्ञेया दश भावाः स्वभावजाः ॥

It is not possible to elaborate these dramatic concepts further in this work. It is our duty to apply the most valuable of these to the modern drama in India while enlarging its scope and range and appeal. In my work on Kalidasa I shall show how we can derive new inspiration and guidance from the classic drama of India in our great task of the future up-building of the Indian stage. The closet drama of India became stiff and modern and convention-ridden beyond measure. The popular drama is a mere piece of transcript from life, a hotchpotch and a medley and nothing more, in which song covers a multitude of artistic sins. The modern amateur stage is yet in leading strings. The drama of mingled prose and song is an artistic solecism but it is one of the legacies—one of the onerous gifts of the popular stage. Side by side with it and while refining and improving it, we must have new and fine and artistic forms of drama. We must evolve in the vernaculars a new and simple verse-form which will be an effective vehicle for the verse-drama. In the world of Tamil letters the *agaval* metre would probably be the best. We must learn from the west to differentiate and yet coordinate the new dramatic forms. We must have ballets and operas and social dramas in prose and tragedies and comedies and farces and historical plays in profusion. Into these must be infused our fundamental aesthetic concepts of *alamkara* and *riti* and *rasa* and *dhvani* so as to breathe life into the dry bones of dramatic forms. Then shall we have fulfilled our aesthetic duty by our motherland by thus revealing India to herself and to the world, and by being enabled, in the words of the greatest dramatist of the world "to hold as it were the mirror up to nature, to show virtue her own feature, scorn her own image and the very age and body of the time his form and pressure".

CHAPTER VIII.

Indian Æsthetics and Indian Erotics.

IT is not as well and as widely known as it deserves to be that the Indian love poetry and the Indian art of love are of exquisite loveliness and charm. Though the modern Indians are on the whole a sad people cut off from their own ideals and festivals and denied the finer festivals of Art in the West, ancient India had an exquisite perception not only of the highest spiritual values of life and of the aesthetic and artistic values, but also of the values and joys of love.

It is not my purpose here to discuss the Indian love poetry in great detail. In it, as in many other branches of the art of poesy, Kalidasa is the supreme master. His *Kumarasambhava* shows the exquisite beginning of love and its still more exquisite completion throughout the austerities of self-denial and self-dedication. His *Raghuvamsa* contains finished portraits of conjugal love and fidelity. His *Ritusamhara* shows the linking of human love with the seasons of nature. In his *Malavikagnimitra* love rules the court and in his *Vikarmorvisiya* love rules earth and heaven. In his *Sakuntala* we see the meeting point of love and devotion, of earth and heaven. But it is in the *Meghasandesa* that we find the most exquisite delineation of love in longing and separation. In the *Amaru Sataka* also we find exquisitely beautiful descriptions of the longings and anticipations and other moods of love. Some of the sweetest love poetry is found also in Bhavabhuti's *Uttararamacharitra*.

But as I stated above I do not desire to stray into those flowery meads. I desire to confine myself to Indian Erotics proper and even here I desire to confine myself to the vital interrelations of Indian Erotics and Indian Aesthetics. I do not attach any importance to the wire-drawn distinctions about the four classes of men *sasa*, *mriga*, *vrisha*, and *asva* (*i.e.*, hare, deer, bull and horse) or the four classes of women (*padmini*, *chitrini*, *sankhini*, and *hastini*. No importance whatever need be attached to such classifications and distinctions. But it is necessary to know and bear in mind the finer aesthetic aspects of love as dealt with in Vatsyayana's *Kamasutras*, *Kuchimara Tantra*, *Ratimanjari*, *Ratirahasya*, *Anangaranga* and other works devoted to erotics. These works are of value and interest not only to devotees of pleasure but also to devotees of aesthetics as well.

Vatsyayana says well that Kama is the fruit of Dharma and Artha (wealth) and that without its attainment the latter are a mere waste of effort. Jayamangala says in his commentary on the sutra, फलभूताश्च धर्मार्थयोः thus:—

सुखार्थं धर्मार्थयोः सेवा। तदसेवायां तौ वन्ध्यभूतौ केवलमायासफलौ स्याताम ॥

(Dharma and Artha are sought for the sake of pleasure. Without the latter they are sterile and have mere vexatious fatigue as their result). Vatsyayana then proceeds to enumerate the 64 *kalas* or arts the knowledge of which is necessary to a right enjoyment of the pleasures of life. Among these are mentioned *Gita* (vocal music), *vadya* (instrumental music), *nrityam* (dancing), *pustakavachanam* (reading poetry), *natakakhyayikadarsanam* (knowledge of dramas and stories), *kavyasamasyapooranam* and *kavyakriya* (power of poetic composition). It is thus clear that the intimate connection of art and love was clearly realised in India. Art without love misses its sweetest purpose, and love without art is mere bestiality. Vatsyayana says well:

कलानां ग्रहणादेव सौभाग्यमुपजायते ।

(The auspiciousness of love is born only through the learning of the arts).

One of the most beautiful Indian ideas is that *Vipralambha Sringara* (love in separation) is more full of charm and attractiveness than love in union (*Sambhoga Sringara*). Bhoja says well in his *Sarasvati Kanthabharana* :

न विना विप्रलम्भेण संभोगो पुष्टिमश्नुते ।
कषायिते हि वस्त्रादौ भूयान् रागो विवर्धते ॥

Sringara is of three kinds *viz*., Ayoga, Sambhoga and Vipralambha (love without fruition, love in union and love in separation). Kalidasa says in his Malavikagnimitra:

अनातुरोत्कण्ठितयोः प्रसिद्धयता
समागमेनापि रतिर्न मां प्रति ।
परस्परप्राप्तिनिराशयोर्वरं
शरीरनाशोऽपि समानुरागयोः ॥

(I do not rejoice in the union of two lovers one of whom is indifferent and the other is passionate. Much higher and sweeter is even the death of two lovers of equal and equally passionate yearning and longing, who are hopeless about the attainment of their desire).

It is thus clear that the inter-relations between Indian Aesthetics and Indian Erotics are interesting and deserve careful study. Both the sciences show a careful study of human nature and a subtle analysis of human emotions. I cannot conclude this chapter better than by quoting a stanza which occurs in Bhanudatta's *Rasamanjari* and which describes the pure and varied emotions of a young and faithful and loving wife.

गतागतकुतूहलं नयनयोरपाङ्गावधि
स्मितं कुलनतभ्रुवामधर एव विश्राम्यति ।
वचः प्रियतमश्रुतेरतिथिरेव कोपक्रमः
कदाचिदपि चेत्तदा मनसि केवलं मज्जति ॥

(The raising and withdrawing of the eyes of a pure and high-souled wife do not travel beyond the ends of the eyes and have no purpose beyond enkindling the love of her husband. Her smile travels not beyond her lips; her words do not go beyond the ears of her lord; her anger is but a rare guest and even if it arises in her heart it sinks again into her pure and loving heart).

CHAPTER IX.

Indian Æsthetics and Indian Arts.

IT will not be possible to deal in this work with the vast subject of Indian arts in any detail. To deal with it adequately will require a separate Volume or each art. I shall however refer briefly to the aspect of the Indian arts as an embodiment and expression of Indiana esthetical ideas.

We should remember that though this work treats only of general aesthetical ideas in India and incidentally treats about their expression in fine art and especially in poetry, the influence of the Indian aesthetical concepts is found in all arts—fine, decorative and industrial. Dr. Ananda Koomaraswami has said well: "Indian design is an inexhaustible treasure-house of fine invention. But have you ever reflected that all this invention belongs to the past, that modern India, anglicised India, has produced no beauty and romance, but has gone far to destroy the beauty and romance which are heritage from the past". Let us take the decorative and industrial art of India. If we carefully study our past achievements in arms and armour, brass and copper wares, carpets, woven stuffs, damascened and inlaid work, enamelling, ivory work, jewelled jade, jewellry, lacquer work, plates, pottery, &c., we find how to mental love of beauty and fine inventiveness was added a wonderful deftness of touch. Even on the simplest articles of daily use the Indian craftsman lavished wonderful loveliness. Yet the Indian poor of today has begun to fetch water in ugly kerosene tins rather than in beautiful pottery or brass vessels. The old fine and fast vegetable dyes have fled :before the loud and blazing aniline and alizarine dyes. Our rich men and zemindars go in for second-rate art rubbish from abroad. Foreign perfumes are preferred to indigeneous perfumes. Our dress has become outlandish. This is not all. Our speech itself has been contaminated. Our architecture is fast becoming a hotch-potch of all sorts of fantastic styles. Our painting is going on erratic courses of its own. The gramaphone and the harmonium have begun to drive out our sweet-toned and expressive musical instruments.

The entire trouble is due to the fact that we, miseducated and misled, do not believe in India's regeneration through art. We think that India's regeneration will come through the polling-booth alone. Political work is all important as it is the basis of everything. But if it is not buttressed by other work in the realms of art and religion, it will fall, and even if it stands it will be a poor show indeed.

Let us think of the situation at least in terms of human sympathy even if we have become incapable of conceiving it in terms of art and aesthetics. The loss of artistic taste and perception among the so-called *literati* and *intelligentsia* in India has resulted in innumerable workers in industrial and decorative and fine arts having been thrown out of work and compelled to press on the industry of agriculture, a crowded field with diminishing returns. What can we say about that blind national suicide which has converted the village weaver into an agricultural labourer and is fast converting the village artizan also into a cooly on the fields ?

The few industrial and decorative artists who still live on are leading degraded and precarious lives without joy in their work and courage in their hearts. The ever-increasing cranks and tourists and curio collectors keep them alive in a state of ill-nourished and joyless life.

The bulk of the workers who have not yet been driven out of their professions into becoming farm-labourers are degrading themselves by giving up their traditional skill and learning and trying to imitate foreign patterns to charm and satisfy the degraded aesthetic tastes of the rich in India. Sir G. Watt says: "Throughout India the fine old art designs that have been attained after centuries of evolution are being abandoned and models utterly unsuited and far inferior artistically are being substituted. The writer can confidently affirm that he found in at least fifty per cent of the important silversmiths' shops in India, the illustrated trade catalogues of European firms and stores being employed as the pattern books upon which their silverplate was being modelled" (*Indian Art at Delhi*). It is well-known that silver trophy articles, nay, silver presents on marriage occasions are all increasingly made according to outlandish designs.

I must not continue this description further because the main purpose of this work lies elsewhere. That a great deterioration has come about is obvious to the most careless observer of things. Even so early as 1879 in an address to Sir George Birdwood signed by William Morris, Edward

Burne Jones, J. E. Millais and others, they referred to "the rapid deterioration that has of late befallen the great historical arts of India". They stated also that "goods which ought to be common in the market are now becoming rare treasures for museums or the cabinets of rich men." Quite recently Mr. H. Wolinski, the Polish artist, stated in a lecture at Bangalore on 27th November 1926, that wealth is not necessary to make a home beautiful, that what is required is a good artistic taste, that handicrafts can bring out the artistic faculty and the colour sense and can supply good and original artistic work, that machinery could never supply it, that handicrafts are being revived in the west while they are being left to perish in India, that even now though deteriorated through the workers introducing foreign dyes and using western designs the handicrafts are still alive in India and should be encouraged, that the Indian nature is very sensitive to colour and design as we know by the charming effects in Indian dress, and that the modern Indian home is singularly lacking in beauty, being either very bare and ugly with little or no attempt at decoration, or as in some of the wealthier homes, filled with foreign articles placed anyhow, without any sense of order or harmony.

The fine arts have had an even worse fate than the industrial and decorative arts. Sir George Birdwood says: "The worst mischief is perhaps done by the architecture foisted on the country by the Government of India, which being the architecture of the state, is naturally thought to be worthy of all imitation". Indian painting was in an equally bad way but is now emerging into new life under the influence of the Bengal school of painting which is, however, threatening to go to the other extreme and sink under the weight of symbolism. In Madras there is neither painting nor any school of painting. In fact in respect of matters of Art Madras is the most philistine portion of India, though the Carnatic style of music, pure and intricate and wonderful, is fighting yet so to say, in the last ditch. Tanjore which was a home of musicians is losing that proud distinction. The Vina-makers of Tanjore like the painters of Tanjore are fast ceasing to exist.

In this lamentable state of artistic decline the aims and ideals and achievements of Indian Art have to be broadcasted throughout the length and breadth of the land. A new surge of love of beauty must fill the national temperament if India is to become once more the home of beauty and romance and happiness and break her present record of ugliness and drabness and unhappiness. In this new campaign of proportion and symmetry and colour and harmony and idealism against maladjustment and deformity and colourlessness and discord and materialism, Aesthetics must be our guide so that art may not become erratic and wayward and lop-sided and endanger the higher values of life.

Indian art, to speak about it in general terms, is both the cause and the effect of Indian Aesthetics. Indian Aesthetics was distilled from Indian Art and was in its turn the perfumer of Indian Art, just as Indian Art was distilled from the Indian temperament and was in its turn the perfumer of the Indian temperament.

The Indian art is essentially creative, idealistic, romantic, devotional and serene. It shows a keen sense of rhythm and sweetness and loveliness. Its keenest and subtlest self-expression is in the realms of *ahimsa* and *santi* and *prema* and *yoga*. These four words are almost untranslateable if we desire to convey the infinite treasure of suggestion which is contained in each word. The realisation and expression of the calm beauty of gods and goddesses with many heads and hands, the soaring temple domes which stand like earth's folded palms uplifted in an ecstasy of worship, the way in which the two great epics surge through misfortune into temporal power and then mellow into calm and peace and renunciation, the golden and vibrant meloncholy of Indian music—these are not mere accidents but are the vital self-expressions of the ideals of India as embodied in the abovesaid four words of wonder and magic and mystery. Even these four words can be compressed into one word *Ananda* or *Rasa* which I have referred to already. It is the touch of the Infinite Bliss that has thrilled Indian thought to the very core and has blossomed into the wonderful Art of India and Aesthetics of India.

Let me elaborate these ideas a little. I have already discussed the concepts of creativeness and idealism and romanticism. Modern art is largely imitative and realistic. It has its place and value in life. In life and in art we must learn a little of the modern mastery of the concrete. But we must not give up our national distinctiveness and surrender our national temperament.

Very probably the modern love of realism in landscape painting is due to concentration in towns leading to the loss of touch with nature's life in the open country as created by God. In a land of villages like India there need not be the same passion for realism in landscape painting. But I am resting the creative and idealistic and romantic trend of Indian Art on a deeper and holier ground. The Indian intellect is divinely dowered with the faculty of insight and introspection. You may call this faculty by the name *yoga* or by any other name. This intuition of the Infinite Beauty and Bliss has been almost an obsession with the Indian mind. The Indian idealisation of the universe and the Indian realisation and expression of the Infinite in and through the finite and of the Divine through the human and the natural are due to this rare faculty of inner vision and superconscious experience. Indian Art relates empirical reality and transcendental reality and thus links Indian philosophy and religion to Indian life in the outer world. Even in expressing outward objects it tries to grasp the elusive idea and express the *norm* or standard of which the object is an expression and to which it is an approximation. It tries to kindle the spark of the ideal in the real by blowing on it with the breath of the Infinite. By such means the real takes fire and while preserving its form and outline becomes warm with a new heat and bright with a new radiance. Thus Indian art frees the Self from the self and reveals Its beauty unto itself. As Goethe has said:

"Each age has sung of beauty—
He who perceives it is from himself set free".

Indian art is not only creative and idealistic and romantic; it is based on *yoga* and spiritual intuition and is hence devotional in its feeling and serene in its expression. It is in moods of "peace that passeth all understanding", when the agitation of the mind is stilled and the inner eye is opened, that the verities of the infinite and eternal world dawn upon our eyes. Then comes the inner urge to sing it in hymns and utter it in philosophy and express it in art. The mysticism and symbolism and transcendentalism of Indian art is due to the Indian faculty of vision and insight and intuition. In India religion and philosophy and art form a trinity in unity and a unity in trinity. This does not mean that nature is neglected or ignored in India. In fact in architecture and sculpture and painting and poetry nature is ominipresent. But nature is linked up with something higher and greater than itself. The Indian mind worked through nature up to Nature's God. The fleeting forms constituting the procession of life were seen in relation to the enduring glory of the Infinite and Inclusive All. The Gods and Goddesses who control and guide the destinies of Nature were visioned and adored and sung and expressed with infinite reverence. *Sukraniti* says: "Let the builder establish images in temples by meditation on the deities who are the objects of his devotion; for the successful achievement of this *dhyana yoga* (yoga of meditation) the nature and characteristics of the divinity are described in sacred works". That is why the Indian sculptor visions his ideal and goes to the actual world for approximations and suggestions. The western sculptor generalises from the actual figures and paints from a model. Deussen asks well: "Why should the artist wish to imitate laboriously and inadequately what nature offers everywhere in unattainable profusion?" Imitation is a delight; but intuition is bliss. Dr. A. K. Koomaraswami says well: "India is wont to suggest the eternal and inexpressible infinities in terms of sensuous beauty. The love of man for woman or for nature are one with his love for God" Sex-love is refined into spiritual love by human life being seen in relation to the life devine. It is the first flash of the realisation of unity. The idea in India has always been not art for art's sake but art for the sake of God.

Indian Architecture has been deservedly famous throughout the world. The Taj in North India and the great temples in South India have struck all with wonder and admiration. Architecture is the Mother Art and is a synthesis of all the arts. In India sculpture and painting were its adherents. The finest flights of poetry and song were due to its influence and inspiration. By allying all the other arts with architecture and by making the temples open to the masses, India democratised art in a wonderful way. It is not proper to describe here the various styles of Indian architecture or to give the history of Indian architecture. My aim is only to show in the finest examples of Indian architecture that combination of massiveness and upwardness which is the soul of Indian Art in general. The art is still a living art though its life is an ebbing life. Fergusson says in his famous *History of Indian and Eastern Architecture*: "Architecture in India is still a living art, practised on the principles which caused its wonderful development in Europe in the twelfth and thirteenth centuries, and there consequently and there alone, the student of architecture has a chance of seeing the real principles of the art in action. In Europe, at the present day, architecture is practised in a manner so anomalous and so abnormal that few, if any, have hitherto been able to shake off the influence of a false system and see that the art of ornamental building can be based on principles of common sense, and that when so practised, the result not only is, but must-be satisfactory". The various *Silpa Sastras* which I have discussed elsewhere contain aphoristic and poetic literature embodying a tradition which is alive to this day. Only a few years ago the *sthapati* or master-builder who built the Nataraja temple at *Tillaivilagam* in the Tanjore District told me that he had as the family heirloom a set of simple Sanskrit verses in regard to architecture and sculpture.

Indian Sculpture and iconography are as valuable as Indian architecture. These Indian arts aimed at visioning the divine form in meditation and then expressing it as realised in vision. Sukracharya says: "The artist should attain the images of the God by means of spiritual contemplation only. The spiritual vision is the best and truest standard for him. He should depend upon it, and not at all upon the visible objects perceived by external senses. It is always commendable for the artist to draw the images of the Gods." The Sculpture in Indian temples abounds not only in representations of Gods but abounds also in representations of human and animal and vegetable forms. The temple pillars and domes are literally filled with sculptural achievements and have a bewildering profusion of sculptural adornment.

European artists and art-critics are unable to realise how a God with many heads or arms can be beautiful. If they can tolerate the nimbus or wings—no human being has ever yet had either—I fail to see why they should be shocked by the Indian vision and expression of divine loveliness. Western art may excel in technique and anatomical knowledge and perspective but Indian art excels in vision and imagination and intuition and creative faculty and need not take with bowed head the chastisements of western art-critics.

Modern Indian Sculpture has to retain the vital *motifs* and methods of ancient Indian sculpture and at the same time widen its range. It has to excel also in human and animal sculpture and in giving concrete outward form to the newborn emotions of patriotism and heroism; and liberty and equality and fraternity surging through the land. It will then become the monument of Indian life at its best and at the same time the living shrine of a living people.

Indian painting also is completely imbued with the fundamental principles and traits of Indian Art in general. It has been said well that the painting of the west is an art of 'mass' while that of the East is an art of 'line'. The western artist delights in landscape painting and in fidelity to nature. The Indian artist does not scorn nature but delights in clear-cut expressions of intuitively realised forms. Leonardo has said well: "A good painter has two chief objects to paint, namely, man and the intention of his soul. The first is easy, and the second difficult because he has to represent it through the attitudes and movements of the limbs." It is in the latter art that we see the speciality and excellence of Indian painting. On the faces of the Indian paintings of divinities, just as on the faces of the Indian sculptures, there broods a benignant peace. Eckhardt says: "Real sanctification consists in this, that the spirit remains immovable and unaffected by all import of love and hate, joy or sorrow, honour or shame, as a huge mountain is unstirred by a gentle breeze. This immovable sanctification causes man to attain the nearest likeness to God he is capable of". As I have said in my recent book on *Tagore—Poet, Patriot and Philosopher* (Sri Vani Vilas Press, Srirangam) "Hence it is that the soaring *gopurams* shining like arms lifted in supplication to God, the indescribable and divine stillness and repose of our painted and sculptured images, and the divine tenderness that breathes through Indian song are all due to the essential characteristics of the Indian genius". The Indian painter expresses the *Rasas* in colours just as the singer expresses them in harmonies and the poet in words.

It may not be out of place to mention here that in the Upanishads there is a reference to a painter's brush: "Let a man with firmness separate the spirit, the inner soul from his own body, as from a painter's brush a fibre". The *Ramayana* refers to painted halls. These mural pictures were the precursers and prototypes of the later picture galleries of Buddhist art like the painted cave temples of Ajanta. The *Mrichchakatika* and *Sakuntala* and

Malavikagnimitra and *Uttara-rama-charita* refer to picture-halls in rich men's houses. In Vatsyayana's *Kama sutras*, we have a reference to the six limbs (*Shadanga*) of painting. These are *rupabheda* which relates to the knowledge of appearances and refers to the study of nature and the knowledge of forms and figures, *pramanam* which means perspective and includes proportion, anatomy, foreshortening, and correctness of measure and structure, *bhava* or the expression of feelings through forms, *lavanya yojanam* or the addition of grace and brightness and splendour, *sadrisyam* or perfect fidelity and truth to the natural and the supernatural as realised in moods of joy enkindled by sight of beauty, and *varnikabhanga* or perfect technique in the use of the brush and the colours and perfect mastery of the implements and materials used in painting. The ancient work *Chitra Lakshana* deals with religious paintings in great detail. In Tamil there is an *Ovianool* (ஓவியநூல்) belonging to the Sangam period and dealing with the art of painting. The ancient Tamil Mahakavyas show what a high standard was attained by painting in South India.

It is not possible to discuss here the details which are characteristic of the Buddhist and the

Rajput and the Moghul and the modern Bengal Schools of painting. Buddhist paintings aimed at visualising the ideals of Buddhisim. Mr. Griffith says of the Ajanta paintings :—"The artists who painted them were giants in execution. Even on the vertical sides of the walls some of the lines which were drawn with one sweep of the brush struck me as being very wonderful; but when I saw long delicate curves drawn without faltering, with equal precision, upon the horizontal surface of a ceiling, where the difficulty of execution is increased a thousandfold it appeared to me nothing less than miraculous". Rajput painting excelled in miniature painting. It delineates the epic and romantic incidents contained in Indian Scriptures. Moghul painting excelled in portraiture and studies of birds and animals. Akbar and Jehangir were great patrons of painting. Akbar said once:—"There are many that hate painting, but such men I dislike. It appears to me as if a painter had quite peculiar means of recognising God, for a painter, in sketching anything that has life, and in devising the limbs one after another, must come to feel he cannot bestow personality upon his work, and is thus forced to thank God, the Giver of life, and will thus increase his knowledge". The recent Ravi Varma School, though it may be deficient in expressing the divine aspects of forms of gods and goddesses and erred in making them too human and too pretty, led the way in choosing Indian subjects and in giving a new channel of expression to the colour sense of the people. In the modern Bengal School headed by Abanindra Nath Tagore and the modern Andhra School headed by the late D. Rama Row, we find a genuine and remarkable attempt to introduce Indian artistic *motifs* and express the genius of Indian art, ideas and art-styles. They aim at making paintings true Indian poems in form and colour and perspective.

I quite realise that we have to add new inspirations to our art. The new-born intensity of interest in man and nature demands a new school of portraiture and landscape painting just as Indian Music has to give scope to the expression of the new fervour of patriotic feeling and Indian poetry has to widen its range of subjects and treatment and expression so as to express also modern life in poetry and drama and include tragedies and historical plays and lyrics of nature and love and patriotism. Thus art is the mirror of the land and of the age and is also the mirror of the eternal things and of the inborn genius of the race. Though the achievements of Indian painting as now extant are perhaps not so wonderful as the achievements of Indian architicture and music and poetry, they are wonderful enough and express the finest and innermost Indian aesthetical ideas and deserve our reverent admiration.

I do not propose to deal with Indian poetry at great length as I have already dealt with Indian aesthetical ideas and Indian rhetoric with special reference to Indian poetry and have also discussed Indian drama and dramaturgy in great detail. It has been well said: "Poetry rules over all in India." Professor Max Dunker says: "The treasures of poetry in India are inexhaustible". In the Vedas we find sudden and perfect outbursts of quintessential poesy. The poet-saints of the Vedas were men of intuition and imagination whose vision was thrilled by loveliness and purified by holiness. Take a verse like the following which occurs in the *Isavasyopanishad*.

हिरण्मयेन पात्रेण सत्यस्यापिहितं मुखम् ।
तत्त्वं पूषन्नपावृणु सत्यधर्माय दृष्टये ॥

(The face of Truth Divine is hidden by the outer golden disc of the sun. Withdraw these blinding rays a while, O Pushan, so that I may have a vision of the Truth Divine).

The Indian epics amplify the declarations of the Vedas in perfect poetry. The next great figure is Kalidasa. In him was summed up one of the greatest epochs of the life of India. Even in the later artificial poetry we have fine flashes. But even finer flashes shine out in individual verses which have passed from hand to hand and from mouth to mouth and many of which are yet uncollected. Let me take one such verse by way of illustration.

श्यामः कटाक्षनिक्षेपाद्गोपीनां नूनमच्युतः ।
तेऽपि पीतांबरध्यानात्पीतिमानं परं ययुः ॥

(Verily is Krishna dark in colour because the dark side-glances of the *gopis* were fixed on him and left there. Because they immediately closed their eyes in meditation of his golden raiment after looking at his person, the golden tint of his raiment filled their being and shone out as the molten gold of their hue).

The beautiful vernaculars of India are not behind Sanskrit in their poetic record. Tulsi Das's Ramayana in Hindi, the hymns of the Maharashtra saints, the poems of the Bengali poets including the great poetic achievement of Rabindranath Tagore, the great poems of Tikanna and Pothanna in Telugu, the ancient Kavyas of Tamil and the Tirukural and Tevaram and Tiruvachakam and Tiruvoimozhi and Kambaramayanam in Tamil form a poetic achievement without parallel in the literature of the world.

But Indian poetry has a yet greater task and a yet higher privilege before it. It has to voice modern India to herself and guide India into the great era of peace and plenty and prosperity and perfection in store for her in the future. The new ideals of liberty and equality and fraternity and patrotism and heroism have to be enshrined in poetry so that they may become a shining light in the national heart. We have to learn from the west directness and brevity and naturalness of utterance. We have to democratise literature so that it will illumine and sweeten the life of the masses. The entire higher knowledge of the west in realms of the real has to filter through Indian literature to the Indian people. All this has to be done without allowing the bloom of the Indian poetry of the past to wither away in the poetry of to-day.

Indian Music also is a flower on the same stem *viz.*, the stem of Indian Art. It was realised in the past in itself and in relation to emotional states and in relation to religion. The modern danger is that it is likely to cut itself away from aesthetic and emotional and religious ideas and revel in mere intricacies of sound. Miss Anne C. Wilson says: "The people of India are an essentially musical race.... It must, therefore, be a secret source of pride to them to know that their system of music, as a written science, is the oldest in the world. Its principal features were given long ago in Vedic writings." The melodies are grouped into *ragas* (masculine) and *raginis* (feminine) and have their appropriate time and season and presiding deities. The *Sama Veda* which is a musical scripture is pronounced by the Lord in Gita as being Himself among the Vedas. The *Gandharvaveda* (the science of music) is reckoned as an *upaveda*. The *Ramayana* was sung by Kusa and Lava; Sarasvati sings on the *vina*; Krishna plays on the flute. The Indian Musical plays are steeped in a musical atmosphere. Even poetry is generally sung in a chant, though in a restrained way. The Bhakti hymns which sprang up like artesian fountains through the outer deserts of disintegrating social and economic and political life brought sweetness and solace to the arid and aching hearts of men. In modern times Tagore has shown the intimate and inalienable alliance of poetry and music and spirituality.

The Indians are not content with tones and semitones but use quartertones and employ a wonderful variety of musical graces. Miss. Wilson says that the Indian has "the most subtle ear for tune" and "an acuteness of musical hearing" (*Hindu* System of Music). Though there is a difference between the Hindustani or northern school of Indian Music and the Karnatic or southern school, they are yet based on the fundamental musical principles stated in *Sangitaratnakara*, *Ragamanjari*, *Raga-Tarangini*, *Chaturdandiprakasika*, *Ragavibodha*, *Sangita Darpana*, *Sangita Parijata*, *Sangita Saramritam*, *Sangita Ragakalpadruma* and other works. The Tamils had a high musical proficiency and an original evolution of music as is clear from the works of Ilankovadigal. The *Paripadal* refers to seven *palais* (musical modes). The *yazh* (யாழ்) was the most famous of the Tamil muscial instruments and was different from the *Vina*, though similar to it. Indian music is the treasure-house wherein are shrined the innermist realities of Indian life and Indian stories and Indian religion.

The Indian musical instruments are of wonderful variety and responsiveness. In the Vedas we find references to such instruments of percussion as *dundubhi* and *adambara* and *bhoomidundubhi* and *Vanaspali* and *aghati*, stringed instruments like *Karkari* and *Vama* and *Vina* and wind instruments like *tunava* and *nadi*. The Yajur Veda refers to lute players and flute players and conch-blowers and drummers. Such an ancient work as the *Rik Pratisakhya* to the *Tara* and *Madhya* and *Mandra* (high and middle and low) octaves and the seven notes of the gamut. The *Ramayana* refers to *bheri, dundubhi, mridanga, pataha, ghata, panava, dindima, adambara, vina* etc.—In the Sundara Kanda Valmiki refers to

शुश्राव मधुरं गीतं त्रिस्थानस्वरभूषितम् ।

(He heard sweet music which was adorned by sounds rising from three loci).

The *Gita* refers to *Sankha, bheri, panava, anaka, gomukha* etc. In the Srimad Bhagavata Narada refers to his Vina thus :

देवदत्तामिमां वीणां ब्रह्मस्वरविभूषिताम् ॥

(This God-given Vina adorned with brahma svara).

Sri Suka in a mood of reflected and recollected ecstacy then says about Narada and his Vina :

अहो देवर्षिर्धन्योऽयं यत्कीर्तिं शार्ङ्गधन्वनः ।
गायन्माद्यन्निदं तन्त्र्या रमयत्यातुरं जगत् ॥

(This divine sage is indeed a happy man full of inner affluence, as he sings the glory of the Lord, and singing gets mad with the love of the Lord, and then fills with the ecstacy of the music of his strings, the weary and joyless world).

We have got not only the great melodies invented and improvised by the great masters of the past but also many local and popular tunes in various parts of India. The great musical poem of *Gita–Govinda* by Jayadeva, the works of the Mogul Court musicians like Tansen and Gopal Naik, and the songs of Chaitanya and Haridas and Mirabai nnd Tulsidas and Pundarika and Namadev and Tukaram and Purandara and Tyagayyar and Govinda Marar and Muthusami Dixitar and Syama Sastri and Patnam Subramania Iyer and Mahavythinathier are among the finest achievements of Indian music.

I shall make a brief reference here to Bharata's

Natya Sastra as it contains the earliest systematic exposition of Indian Music (vide chapters 28 to 37), though I am going to refer to it later on in connection with Indian dancing. It refers to stringed instruments (Tata ततं), drums and other instruments of percussion (अवनद्ध), cymbal (घनं), and wind instruments (सुषिर). The generic name is Atodya (आतोद्य). The work gives detailed exposition of *svaras*, *srutis*, *gramas*, *murchanas*, *jatis* etc. Song and instrumental music and dance must whirl round like a lighted torch.

एवं गीतं च वाद्यं च नाट्यं च विविधाश्रयम् ।
अलातचक्रप्रतिमं कर्तव्यं नाट्ययोक्तृभिः ॥

The sage says further what sounds are appropriate to the various *rasas*. He says with keen perception that the voice of women is by nature sweet and that they should take to vocal music and that men should take to instrumental music.

प्रायेण तु स्वभावात् स्त्रीणां गानं नृणां च वाद्यविधिः ।
स्त्रीणां स्वभावमधुरः कण्ठो नृणां सुलालितत्वं च ॥

ये स्त्रीणां पाठ्यगुणो भवति नराणां च गानमधुरत्वम् ।
ज्ञेयोऽलंकारोऽसौ न हि स्वभावो ह्ययं तेषाम् ॥

In regard to the alleged melancholy of

Indian music I may here refer to Mrs. Mann's opinion: "I am often told that all Indian music is melancholy. How can I convey to you that spirit which is sad yet without pain? That is the delicious melancholy of Indian music. Can a lover be joyful away from his beloved? Can a musician sing joyfully, really joyfully, whilst he wanders on this earth? Would it not be sorrow if he forgot his exile? Is not the remembrance of the face of the beloved more dear, though fraught with the pain of separation?"

I take the liberty of quoting once again from my work an *Rabindranath Tagore: Poet, Patriot and Philosopher* (Sri Vani Vilas Press, 1924): "The melodic types vitalized by the spirit of joyful improvisation (*Manodharma*) gave ample scope for the exercise of the highest musical imagination. The Indian instruments of music have combined volume of sound with responsiveness to the soul of the musician. The divine tenderness that is at once the cause and the inspiration of the poignant melancholy of Indian music which is only the quivering of the wings of the soaring soul of spiritual idealism has the same source and origin as the ecstacies of Prema Bhakti and the tranquilised bliss of thought in Yoga...... If the serene sanctities of worship in the homes and the glorious pageants of worship in the temples cease to be facts and inspirations, then will begin the decline and downfall of Indian music. In the past of India music and religion went hand in hand like Shakti and Siva—two yet one, diverse in beauty and yet single in soul. Music in India took up life in its fulness, relieved the monotony of toil, sweetened the pleasures of domestic festivities, soothed the sorrows of the sick, inspired the joys of the artist, and uplifted the soul of the devotee to the lotus feet of God".

I do not for a moment say that Indian music should rest on its laurels. It has to root itself in the past and yet meet the present age in all its manifoldness and usher in the great future that is to be. It must add the delights of harmony and choir music without sacrificing its distinctive emphasis on melody. Indian melody is produced by the regulated development of concordant notes while western harmony is produced by the concord of many related notes. Indian music is so to say one-dimensional while its western music is two-dimensional. The *crescendo* and *descrescendo* of sound, along with *gamakas* (graces), within the *raga* limits, have wonderful charm. The showered cluster of notes in harmony has an appeal of its own. We can certainly achieve an Indian musical exposition of the spirit of harmony. We have also to expand the range of our music so as to include the new-born moods of heroism and patriotism and freedom. Well has it been said that "the song that nerves a nation's heart is in itself a deed".

I shall, however, deal in some detail with the arts of dancing and acting because they are connected with æsthetics and with the arts of poetry and drama and music intimately and also because in modern India they have fallen into oblivion because they have got mixed up with questions of social reform. The expression of *rasa* is its primary object and its instrument is the wonderful and expressive human body aided by the enchantments of look and the magic of tone and the beauty of gesture. Kalidasa says about it in the *Malavikagnimitra*:

नाट्यं भिन्नरुचेर्जनस्य बहुधाप्येकं समाराधनम्

(It is the one common means of delight of men of diverse temperaments).

Bharata's *Natya Sastra* is a very remarkable and valuable work not only in respect of *rasa* and dramaturgy but also in respect of dancing as well.

It describes the construction of the dancing hall (Rangamantapa), and the worship of the deities there. (Rangadaivatapujavidhana). It then describes elaborately the nature of Tandava. I may state here that *Nritya* is the pantomimic representation of feeling (Bhava) and *Nritta* consists of the movements of the body with gestures and is regulated by *Tala* (the marking of time or musical interval). Nritya is called Marga and Nritta is called *Deshi*. Dancing is divided into *Tandava* (vigorous dancing) and *lasya* (gentle dancing), the presiding deities of which are Siva and Parvati. Kalidasa refers to this in his verse in Malavikagnimitra where he says :

रुद्रेणदमुमाकृतव्यतिकरे स्वाङ्गे विभक्तं द्विधा ।

(Rudra by his union with Uma in his person has divided it in two aspects in his person).

It is further stated that the appropriate modes of dancing in relation of sringara (love), vira (heroism) and hasya (the comic) are *churita* (चुरित), laghunritya and Vikata. It is stated also that Siva and Parvati taught twenty varieties of Marga dancing and Sixteen varieties of Desi dancing.

To proceed with the great work of Bharata, he describes *Poorvaranga* (prologue) and then deals elaborately with *rasas*. He says :

न हि रसादृते कश्चिदर्थः प्रवर्तते ।

(Without rasa, no purposeful meaning ensues).

" यथा बहुद्रव्ययुतैर्व्यञ्जनैर्बहुभिर्युतम् ।
आस्वादयन्ति भुञ्जाना भक्तं भक्तविदो जनाः ॥
भावाभिनयसंबद्धान्स्थायिभावांस्तथा बुधाः ।
आस्वादयन्ति मनसा तस्मान्नाट्यरसाः स्मृताः ॥
न भावहीनोऽस्ति रसो न भावो रसवर्जितः ।
परस्परकृता सिद्धिस्तयोरभिनये भवेत् ॥
व्यञ्जनौषधिसंयोगो यथान्नं स्वादुतां नयेत् ।
एवं भावा रसाश्चैव भावयन्ति परस्परम् ॥
यथा बीजाद्भवेद्वृक्षो वृक्षात्पुष्पं फलं यथा ।
तथा मूलं रसाः सर्वे ततो भावा व्यवस्थिताः ॥

Thus the relish of emotion is similar to the relish of food but the joy belongs to a higher plane. *Rasa* is the seed of which the emotions are the developments. The emotion fills the mind and thrills the body.

योऽर्थो हृदयसंवादी तस्य भावो रसोद्भवः ।
शरीरं व्याप्यते तेन शुष्ककाष्ठमिवाग्निना ॥

The 7th chapter where the expression of feelings is described is of the higest value and shows wonderful subtlety and insight. The 8th and 9th chapters deal with *abhinaya* or gesture. The later chapters deal with dancing. The 15th chapter describes prosody. The 16th chapter deals with alamkaras (figures of speech). The 18th chapter deals with the *dasa rupas* (ten dramatic types). Chapter 20 deals with *Vrittis*. *Abhinaya* is of four varieties: (1) आंगिक or conveyed by bodily action ; (2) वाचिक or conveyed by speech; or (3) आहार्य or conveyed by dress, decoration etc., and (4) सात्विक or conveyed by the manifestation of feelings. Chapter 21 deals with Aharya Abhinaya elaborately. Chapter 22 deals with Samanya Abhinaya. Chapter 25 deals with Chitra Abhinaya. The later chapters in the work deal with music as stated already.

Bharata's work is a mine of ideas and later writers have gone to it for inspiration and guidance in an abundant measure. It describes the Natya Veda as *Vedasammita* or harmonious and concordant with the Veda. It says that Indra and others told Brahma that they wanted a plaything which could be seen and heard so that the selfish and passion-ridden world may be pleasantly and almost unconsciously educated into sweetness and light. They asked for means of delight and uplift and purification and illumination which would be open to all irrespective of caste or creed.

महेन्द्रप्रमुखैर्देवैरुक्तः किल पितामहः ।
क्रीडनीयकमिच्छामो दृश्यं श्रव्यं च यद्भवेत् ॥

न च वेदविहारोऽयं संश्राव्यः शूद्रजातिषु ।
तस्मात्सृजापरं वेदं पञ्चमं सार्ववर्णिकम् ॥

Bharata aays that then Brahma created Natya Veda taking words from Rig Veda, songs from Sama Veda, gesticulation from Yajurveda, and *rasa* from Atharva Veda.

जग्राह पाठ्यं ऋग्वेदात्सामभ्यो गीतमेव च ।
यजुर्वेदादभिनयान् रसानथर्वणादपि ॥

Bharata says further dance and drama are the means by which, through the beautiful and appealing expression of universal feelings, righteousness and self-control and heroism and love will be engendered in the minds of men and women. They will convey a real knowledge of life and superlife. They will satisfy the impulses of play and pleasure. They will soften the asperities of life. Whatever exists or ought to exist can be pourtrayed by them.

धर्मोधर्मप्रवृत्तानां कामाः कामार्थसेविनाम् ।
निग्रहं दुर्विनीतानां मत्तानां दमनक्रिया ॥

अबोधानां विबोधश्च वैदग्ध्यं विदुषामपि ।
ईश्वराणां विलासश्च स्थैर्यं दुःखार्दितस्य च ।
सर्वोपजीविनामर्थो धृतिरुद्विग्नचेतसाम् ॥

नानाभावोपसंपन्नं नानावस्थान्तरात्मकम् ।
लोकवृत्तानुकरणं नाट्यमेतन्मया कृतम् ॥

उत्तमाधममध्यानां नराणां कर्मसंश्रयम् ।
हितोपदेशजननं नाट्यमेतन्मया कृतम् ॥

दुःखार्तानां श्रमार्तानां शोकार्तानां तपस्विनाम् ।
विश्रान्तिजननं काले नाट्यमेतन्मयाकृतम् ॥

धर्म्यं यशस्यमायुष्यं हितं बुद्धिविवर्धनम ।
लोकोपदेशजननं नाट्यमेतद्भविष्यति ॥

न तच्छ्रुतं न तच्छिल्पं न सा विद्या न सा कला ।
नासौ योगो न तत्कर्म यन्नाट्येऽस्मिन्न दृश्यते ॥

योऽयं स्वभावो लोकस्य सुखदुःखसमन्वितः ।
सोऽङ्गाद्यभिनयोपेतो नाट्यमित्यभिधीयते ॥

वेदविद्येतिहासानामर्थानां परिकल्पनम् ।
विनोदकरणं लोकेनाट्यमेतद्भविष्यति ॥

The above beautiful verses apply appositely not only to dancing but to all the fine arts of India. The fine arts, and in an equal measure, the industrial and decorative arts, of India show a keen sense of beauty and ornamentation and feeling and also a subtle and exquisite taste. They show that the highest and finest aesthetic ideas of India were always kept in view by the poets and artists in India and that they anxiously endeavoured to conform to them without losing that distinctive touch of originality which alone gives value to every work of art. At the same time they paid unceasing and heartfelt homage to the highest spiritual ideals of India. They were never influenced by the heresy of art for art's sake. Art can never have a value independent of human delight and Godward devotion. It was by this rare and radiant combination of aesthetics and art and spirituality that India was able to achieve such a unique and honoured place in the universal festival of arts.

CHAPTER X.

Indian Æsthetics and Indian Metaphysics.

WE are now reaching the higest aspect of our subject. In the ascending scale of life's values aesthetics is nearest to metaphysics, though yet far below. In art we see the prism of the higher mind breaking up the white light of the bliss of the soul into the many-coloured radiance of beauty. The claim of aestheticians that the bliss of art is of the same genus as the bliss of the soul is by no means an extravagant claim. It is creative, of the essence of joy, self-dependent, and so intense as to shut out all other intruding lower pleasures and pains. It is, like the bliss of the soul, विगलितवेद्यान्तरं आनन्दं to use the words of Mammatacharya.

I have already shown how the concept of *rasa* is fundamental in Indian Aesthetics and in Indian Metaphysics. '*Rasa*' is satisfaction. The word is primarily applied to the various aspects of taste which are enjoyed by the tongue which is the organ of taste. Sri Sankaracharya says in his famous bhashya on the Taittiriya upanishad:

'रसो नाम तृप्तिहेतुरानन्दकरो मधुराम्लादिप्रसिद्धो लोके ।

(In the world *rasa* is well-known to be the means of satisfaction and the cause of pleasure like sweet, sour etc.).

The annotation of *rasa* in the physical realm has been carried to the super-physical realm in the mental plane of aesthetical realisation and in the supra-mental plane of metaphyscial realisation. Another meaning of the word is essence or juice or water. Take for instance the use of the word in the sense of water in Kalidasa's verse :

सहस्रगुणमुत्स्रष्टुमादत्ते हि रसं रविः ॥

(The sun takes water up as vapour only to return it with thousand-fold usefulness and value).

In the Gita verse

पुष्णामि चौषधीः सर्वा सोमो भूत्वा रसात्मकः ।

(I, becoming the Moon whose soul is the rasa, nourish all the medicinal herbs and plants).

the principle of growth and taste and sweetness is emphasised. Sri Sankaracharya says that the moon who is the abode of all *rasas* vivifies all grains and medicinal plants with growth and sweetness and tastefulness (पुष्टिमति रसस्वादुमति च). We may also remember in this connection that Rasa Sastra means the science of alchemy and the science of chemistry. A well-known stanza says :

यथासिद्धरसस्पर्शादयोऽपि स्वर्णतां व्रजेत् ॥

(Just as by the touch of Rasa even iron becomes gold).

It was quite natural to raise the concept of *rasa* from the plane of physical enjoyment which is after all a gross form of enjoyment. We meet in the history of languages with many instances of elevations and depressions of words. Here is an instance of an unceasing elevation of a word to the loftiest height to which the mind of man can attain.

The ideas of sweetness, tastefulness, satisfation, essence and alchemy which are connoted by the word *rasa* in the plane of physical enjoyment were given the first extension by applying them to family and domestic relations. When man was no longer a mere slave of his physical appetites and when he found a keen satisfaction and delight and sweetness in the purer and less corporeal pleasures of family affection, *rasa* was used to mean such satisfaction. Kalidasa says:

ममात्र भावैकरसं मनः स्थिरं न कामवृत्तिर्वचनीयमीक्षते ।

(My mind which is full of one *rasa* due to affection is rooted in him. The course of love cares not for blame).

इष्टे वस्तुन्युपचितरसाः प्रेमराशीभवन्ति ।

(The rasas or affections augmented in relation to a beloved object become a storehouse of love).

Bhavabhuti speaks of the ripe and deep love of husband and wife thus in his *Uttararamacharita.*

यत्र जरसा यस्मिन्नहार्यो रसः ।

(in which the sweetness is not displaced by advancing age).

But very soon the spirit of man found keener delight and satisfaction and sweetness in the ideal realm of Art than in the realm of ordinary matter-of-fact human life. The manifestation of *rasa* in art adds a wondrous grace to art, and through art adds a yet more wondrous grace to life. Anandavardhana points out this important aspect of *rasa* when he says in the fourth *udyota* familiar things put on a new aspect of glory by the manifestation of rasa just as in the spring trees put on a new and lovely and fragrant bloom. This idea is the same as the idea of poesy as described by Wordsworth and Coleridge in their immortal preface to their "Lyrical Ballads" *viz.*, naturalising the supernatural and supernaturalising the natural.

But this process of the heightening of the meaning of the word could not and did not stop at any point lower than the highest peak of significance—the very *Kailasa* of spiritual bliss. That is the meaning of the words already discussed by me in Chapter X:

रसो वै सः रसं ह्येवायं लब्ध्वानन्दी भवति ।

I have already referred to the three *gunas* and the five *Kosas.* All nature is divisible into three states of being: sattva (equipoise), rajas (activity) and tamas (inertia). The Lord says in the Gita that *sattva* is the pure and effulgent and illumining and happy state of mind and binds the soul to the universe in bonds of knowledge and bliss.

तत्र सत्त्वं निर्मलत्वात्प्रकाशकमनामयम् ।
सुखसंगेन बध्नाति ज्ञानसङ्गेन चानघ ॥

Sri Madhusoodana Sarasvati explains *Nirmala* thus: चिद्बिम्बग्रहणयोग्यत्वात् (ability to receive the image of *chit* or divine consciousness). In art *sattva* predominates and the mind has clarity and illumination and emotional joy and can receive and reflect the image of divine bliss. But even in it the mind is bound to the world in bonds of clear knowledge and sweet delight and we do not have the bliss of spiritual realisation in itself.

We must remember in connection with this the doctrine of the five *Kosas* to which I have already referred above. In art as we grow higher and higher therein we reach the *Vignanamaya Kosa* and the *Anandamaya Kosa.* The grosser sheaths of life are no longer impediments to our full self-expression. By the aid of clear vision and imagination and intuition we realise the innermost truth of things and behold the beauty of creation and enjoy it in bliss and seek to create it in and through the fine arts.

Indian philosophy points out that sound (sabda) has four stages:—Sukshma, Pasyanti, Madhyama and Vaikhari. The *Sukshma* or *para* (subtle) manifestation is luminous and eternal and is said to reside between the seat of the Prana and the seat of the Apana and to be realisable in meditation. गुह्ये षोडशकले तामाहुरमृतां कलाम् । Of this *Sabda Brahma* the next manifestation is *Pasyanti* which is luminous and self-conscious. The next manifestation is *Madh-*

yama which is conceptual but not yet in the form of uttered sounds. The final manifestation by vocal organs or musical instruments etc., is uttered sound (*vaikhari*).

The Veda says:

चत्वारि वाक्परिमिता पदानि तानि विदुर्ब्राह्मणा ये
मनीषिणः ।
गुहा त्रीणि निहिता नेङ्गयन्ति तुरीयं वाचो मनुष्या
वदन्ति ॥

In Bhoja's Sarasvatikantabharana the very first benedictory verse says:

ध्वनिर्वर्णाः पदं वाक्यमित्यास्पदचतुष्टयम् ।
यस्याः सूक्ष्मादिभेदेन वाग्देवीं तामुपास्महे ॥

It seems to me that Sri Sankaracharya's fundamental doctrine of the one Supreme Existence on which the relative manifoldness of the Cosmos is superimposed has unconsciously influenced the origin and development of the concept of *Rasa* and *Dhvani*. The great aestheticians point out that in the sweet realisation of aesthetic *rasa* there are, as in the sweeter realisation of spiritual rasa, the qualities of the exclusion of the disturbing worldliness and the release of the bliss-aspect (*Anandamsa*) of the soul by breaking down what obscures its self-expression (*Avarana bhanga*). But in aesthetic *rasa* the bliss of the soul is coloured and thereby obscured by *rati* (love) etc., which are feelings and emotional states experienced in many births whereas in spiritual *rasa* the bliss of the soul shines forth as it is and unfragmented and unobcsured. Jagannatha Pandita says in his famous work *Rasagangadhara*

अलौकिकेन व्यापारेण तत्कालनिवर्तितानन्दांशावरणाज्ञानेन अत एव प्रमृष्टपरिमितप्रमातृत्वादिनिजधर्मेण प्रमात्रा स्वप्रकाशतया वास्तवेन निजस्वरूपानन्देन सह गोचरीक्रियमाणः प्राग्निविष्टवासनारूपः रत्यादिरेव रसः।

(Rasa is that blissful emotion of rati or love etc., which is of the nature of antenatal Vasanas or emotional tendencies and which is realised through the sheaths of such Vasanas along with the inalienable and internal and self-luminous bliss of the soul and which results from the trancendence of limited cognition and ratiocination by the liberation of the Ananda or bliss-element of the Soul by the aesthetic energising which is different in its nature from the mere energy of worldliness).

He says further:

भग्नावरणचिद्विशिष्टो रत्यादिस्थायिभावो रसः।
रत्याद्यवच्छिन्ना भग्नावरणा चिदेव रसः॥

(Rasa is that shining forth of the bliss of the soul when the barriers to its self-expression are removed, the bliss being expressed through love and other emotional states).

These *sutra-like* statements declare that the soul's *Sacchidananda* nature freed from the veil of worldliness and pain and revelling in the ideal realm of aesthetic delight and expressed in the aesthetic emotions of *rati* (love) etc., is rasa. The white light of the soul is thus refracted by the prism of aesthetic enjoyment into the glorious many-tinted radiances of *rati* (love) etc. This realm of coloured light is higher, sweeter and brighter far than the life of worldiness, with its sense-pleasures which are shadowed by pain and grief. Thus aesthetic *rasa* is different from spiritual rasa in that in the former the consciousness and bliss of the soul (*Chidanandarasa*) expresses itself not in its natural and self-luminous glory but through the sheaths of *rati* (love) and other aesthetic emotions. The word *rasa* applies to both. The description in Chapter VI verse 21 of the Gita :

सुखमात्यन्तिकं यत्तद्बुद्धिग्राह्यमतीन्द्रियम् ।

(that extreme bliss which can be grasped by the mind and which is beyond the senses) applies to both. But there is also the above-said difference between them. In short aesthetic rasa is the sweet lunar glory which is the solar glory softened by being reflected by the lunar art which fills our eyes and minds with sweetness, rapture, and peace.

Thus the aesthetic delight is a reflected bliss (प्रतिबिंबितानन्द). The higher manifestations or *vibuthis* of God in the universe, such as are described in Chapter X of the Gita, charm and fire our vision and imagination and intuition and by such impact there is a breaking down of the barriers to the self-expression of the soul and the joy of the soul pours out through the channels of emotional states (*Bhavas*) into its expresssion in the fine arts. We realise the aesthetic joy at its highest in the highest poesy and music. In the realm of worldly life the ascent of pleasure is from the pleasure of the palate to the pleasure of amorous love. In the gamut of worldly pleasure there are some elements of such reflected delight. In the next higher octave of aesthetic pleasure there are higher elements of such delight. In every such manifestation there must be at least a temporary cessation of desire. Desire and delight can never go together.

Hence it is that art is "emotion recollected in tranquillity," to quote the beautiful remark of Wordsworth. Achyutaraya says in his *Sahityasara* that the Ananda (Bliss) is reflected in the calm surface of such tranquillised emotion as the full loveliness of a beautiful woman is reflected in a pure and polished mirror (Chapter IV verse 19). That is the reason why while worldly pain is so distasteful, aesthetic pain is *Karuna Rasa* and is a source of welcome delight. Visvanatha says well in his *Sahityadarpana.*

सत्त्वोद्रेकादखण्डस्वप्रकाशानन्दचिन्मयः ।
वेद्यान्तरस्पर्शशून्यो ब्रह्मानन्दसहोदरः ॥
लोकोत्तरचमत्कारप्राणः कैश्चित्प्रमातृभिः ।
स्वाकारवदभिन्नत्वेनायमास्वाद्यते रसः ॥
रजस्तमोभ्यामस्पृष्टं मनः सत्त्वमिहोच्यते ॥

(Rasa which, by reason of the predominance of sattvaguna is full of limitless and spontaneous and self-luminous consciousness and bliss, which is free from the taint of intruding objects, which is akin to Brahmic bliss, whose life is supreme and super-worldly and exquisite charm, is enjoyed in a state of union of enjoyer and enjoyed by fortunate and happy discerners of delight. Sattva is the state of the mind which is free from Rajas and Tamas).

Dhananjaya says in Dasarupaka (IV, 43).

स्वादः काव्यार्थसंभेदादात्मानन्दसमुद्भवः ।
विकासविस्तरक्षोभविक्षेपैः स चतुर्विधः ॥

(The aesthetic enjoyment is born of Atmananda and is either a state of expansion and blossoming or a state of elation and elevation or a state of agitation or a state of confusion).

The two words mentioned above—*Brahmasvadasahodarah* and *Atmanandasamudbhava*—contain the essence of the inter-relations of Indian aesthetics and Indian Metaphysics. The aesthetic bliss is a derivative of spiritual bliss and is akin to it but is a coloured prismatic radiance splitting up the white radiance of the spirit by refracting it through the prism of the emotional states. To use the wonderful words of Shelley :

"Art like a dome of many-coloured glass
Stains the white radiance of Eternity."

The difference among *rasa* in the plane of physical enjoyment, *rasa* in the plane of aesthetic enjoyment, and *rasa* in the plane of spiritual enjoyment is a difference of *kosa* or *avarana* or sheath. In the *Annamaya kosa* and *Pranamaya kosa* (the physical sheath and the sheath of energy) the medium is dense. It is more tenuous in the *Manomaya and Vignanamaya kosas* (the lower mental sheath and the higher mental sheath). It is very transparent in the Anandamaya kosa (the sheath of bliss). But the real nature of the Supreme can be expressed properly not so much as Anandamaya as Ananda, not so much as Rasamaya as Rasa. The following scriptural passages show this truth clearly :

को ह्येवान्यात्कः प्राण्यात् । यदेष आकाश आनन्दो न स्यात् । एष ह्येवानन्दयाति ॥

सैषानन्दस्य मीमांसा भवति ।
एतमानन्दमयमात्मानमुपसंक्रामति ।
आनन्दं ब्रह्मणो विद्वान् न बिभेति कुतश्चन ।
आनन्दो ब्रह्मेति व्यजानात् ॥

एतस्यैवानन्दस्याऽन्यानि भूतानि मात्रामुपजीवन्ति ॥

In the *Lalita Trisati* the Devi is called *Ekarasa.* In the *Lalita Sahasranama* the Devi is called as Rasya and also as—

कलानिधिः काव्यकला रसज्ञा रसशेवधिः ।

In his immortal *bhashya* on the Vedanta Sutras I, 1, 12–19, Sankaracharya has elaborated this concept of Ananda with a wonderful wealth of argument and illustration. In his *bhashya* on the Taittiriya Upanishad, Brahmanandavalli, 7th anuvaka, he asks how it is that seekers after the spiritual bliss, although they have no outward means or implements of enjoyment and although they have not even any desire or hankering for enjoyment, are full of gladness even more than persons who have attained worldly pleasures through worldly means. He replies: नूनब्रह्मैव रसस्तेषां। तस्मादस्ति तेषां आनन्दकारणं रसवद्ब्रह्म। (Brahma is their Rasa. To them Brahma which is Rasa is the cause of their bliss). Then all ignorance and desire and action vanish and perfect peace is attained. In that still lake of the mind the full moon of the spiritual Rasa or Ananda (Bliss) is reflected in all its beauty and radiance.

In the Bhagawad Gita (II 60) the Lord says that Rasa will vanish when Para (God) is realised. The Lord contrasts there desire and bliss. Thus mere worldly pleasure is of the nature of soul entanglement and God-obscuration. But aesthetic pleasure involves elements of purity and peace and dispassion and is hence unlike worldly pleasure and hence does not obscure the self-luminous bliss of the soul. The supreme example is that of Valmiki. It wa in his mood of divinest compassion after previous and preparatory piety and austerity and on a holy morning after ablution and worship that poetry was born from pity. Thus æsthetic joy is more akin to spiritual bliss than to worldly pleasure. It is not of the nature of Brahmasamsparsa and Brahma Yoga (touch with God and union with God), described in Chapters VI, 28 and V, 21, and the bliss is not eternal or infinite (*Akshaya and Atyanta*). But it is pure, disinterested, intense and exquisite and is superior to worldly pleasure.

I must now desist from the temptation of discussing this interesting aspect of æsthetics further. Kalidasa suggests in his *Sakuntala* that Sakuntala is partly of human and partly of divine origin, and that even the human origin shows that she was born of *tapas* (austerity). He suggests that Art like Sakuntala has such a wonderful ancestry and is the result of human purity and divine loveliness. न प्रभातरलं ज्योति-रुदेति वसुधातलात् (A radiance full of quivering with splendour does not arise from the earth).

In chapter II I showed how the Brihadaranyaka upanishad passage seeks the aid of human affection to shadow forth the love divine. I. shall in conclusion refer to a beautiful stanza of Bhavabuthi which, like Kalidasa's description of Sakuntala expresses the essence of art and at the same time uses in describing human beauty words which are particularly appropriate to spirituality,

> संभूयेव सुखानि चेतसि परं भूमानमातन्वते
> यत्रालोकपथावतारिणि रतिं प्रस्तौति नेत्रोत्सवः ।
> यद्बालेन्दुकलोच्चयादवचितैः सारैरिवोत्पादितं
> तत्पश्येयमनङ्गमङ्गलगृहं भूयोऽपि तस्या मुखम् ॥

(When shall I see again her face which seems to accumulate all the separate joys of life into a whole and causes a supreme elation and expansion and elevation of the spirit, which, when it approaches the line of vision, creates the bliss born of the festival of the eyes, which seems to have been created out of the essence distilled from the beams of the young and newborn moon, and which is the auspicious abode of love),

The vital words used in this stanza viz., परं भूमानं, रति, सारैः, and अनङ्गमङ्गलगृहं express four important aspects of Art and Aesthetic delight. Such delight causes an elation and expansion and elevation of the mind. It causes deep and intense and exquisite bliss. It is of the essence of life. It is a disembodied and auspicious bliss. In all these respects it is higher than worldly pleasure and is akin to spiritual bliss. It is thus beyond doubt that it is in the fitness of things that æsthetic delight and spiritual bliss are expressed by the same beautiful and expressive word *Rasa*.

CHAPTER XI.

Indian Æsthetics and Indian Education : Conclusion.

AFTER thus discussing Indian Aesthetics from various aspects, I wish in conclusion to plead for giving Indian Aesthetics and Indian Arts their proper place in the scheme of Indian education. By our neglect of them we have done infinite harm already. We have killed the taste of the rich and the livelihood of the poor. We have brought down the level of India's aesthetic conception and artistic achievement. We have degraded India in the eyes of the world. From being a palace of art and beauty and romance she has become a land of inartistic and joyless ugliness.

We must first of all get over that hypnotism which has come ever us and made us think that India was never a home of beauty. That is the unkindest cut of all. Books like that pernicious work—Archer's *India and the Future*—have hypnotised us. I have tried in my work on *Hindu Culture* to remove a general misapprehension about the aims and ideals of Hindu culture. In the realm of art we must try to understand the aims and ideals of Indian Art aright. For the achievements of this result we have to undo the mischief wrought by books belittling Indian Art and get out of that state of hypnotism and stupor and self-contempt into which we had fallen in regard to the arts of India.

The ordinary Indian student knows little Indian history and less Indian philosophy. But the comparative has no application so far as Indian Art and Aesthetics are concerned. He does not know them at all. New universities are growing up everywhere in India. But each new university is a mere copy of its predecessors. In none of them is an attempt made to generate a new manliness, a new loveliness, a new godliness. Sir George Birdwood has said well: "Our education has destroyed their love of their own literature, the quickening soul of a people and their delight in their own arts, and worst of all their repose in their own traditional and national religion. It has disgusted them with their own homes, their parents, their sisters, their very wives. It has brought discontent into every family so far as its baneful influences have reached."

It is by a reform of Indian education by including Indian Art and Aesthetics throughout the course that the real uplift of India will come. We are today a sad people on the whole. Unless we counterbalance external depression by an internal buoyancy we are doomed indeed. Our inner buoyancy and radiance must be so intensified that we shall by their power evercome outer depression and gloom. We must be reborn again in beauty and in bliss.

For this we must pour forth new and vital literature on Art and Aesthetics. We must have primers and advanced books on those subjects. We must make our boys and girls rooted in a new sense of the loveliness of things. In our Universities chairs of Arts and Aesthetics should be endowed. A new stir of passion for the beautiful must vibrate throughout the length and breadth of the land. Indian Art must utter India to herself before it utters India to the world.

This is necessary not for the sake of the cultured classes alone. We all talk today about the world-movement towards democracy. But what is democracy worth without an enlightened and happy people?

If we wish to carry light and love into the hearts of the people, there is no means so effective and universal as Art. Sister Nivedita has said well: "There is no voice like that of Art to reach the people. A song, a picture, these are the fiery cross that reaches all the tribes, and makes them one". We all cry ourselves hoarse with cries about the lack of Indian unity. It is Art that must and will and can bring the gift of concord and harmony.

For the spread of Art and Aesthetics among the people it is not enough to coordinate Indian Art and Aesthetics and Indian Education. We must co-ordinate Indian Art and Indian life by having art galleries in temples and town halls in all the towns in the land. Even in schools we must have demonstration and model rooms showing the arts and handicrafts of India. There must also be in every important centre permanent art show rooms as well as frequent art exhibitions which would conserve old types and achievements and stimulate fresh efforts in arts and handicrafts.

I must now bring this fascinating study of Indian Æsthetics to a close. Whether it will create in my countrymen a new self-realisation in beauty and bliss I do not know. But it has been a source of delight and devotion to me and nothing will give me a greater pleasure than to know that it has won even one worshipper in the shrine of Art and Æsthetics in India. I cannot conclude this volume better than by quoting the following two beautiful lines which contain the quintessence of beauty and blessedness and delight and devotion and which describe that supreme unity of bliss whence proceeds the trinity of beauty, goodness and truth.

रसो वै सः रसं ह्येवायं लब्ध्वाऽनन्दीभवति ॥

(He is Rasa. Attaining Rasa he becomes full of bliss).

कलानिधिः काव्यकला रसज्ञा रसशेवधिः ॥

(She is the mine of the arts. She is the art of poesy. She is the knower of Rasa. She is the supreme treasure-house of Rasa).

ERRATA.

PAGE	LINE	FOR	READ.
7	22	alance	balance
15	19	materials	materials,
17	15	*Ethetique*	*Esthetique*
,,	25	it	is
20	15	J. F. Seeley	J. R. Seeley.
41	5	mere	merely
46	25	variegated	variegated ;
47	2	madhuni	madhuni,
,,	4	beauty Sri	beauty Sri,
48	3	into	of
,,	5	mind	mind,
51	15	*Prakasa*	*Prakasa* :
,,	24	Rasa having	Rasa. Having
64	15	प्रमुक्तः	प्रयुक्तः
78	21	an	on
79	2	*jurta*	*jivita*
,,	12	samsa parya-	samsa, parya-
,,	,,	yoktha	yokti
,,	15	skillful	skilful

PAGE	LINE	FOR	READ.
88	4	*chaitra*	*chitra.*
92	10	only,	only
93	7	gate.	gate,
103	4	omit	æsthetic
104	24	Vibhavas	Vibhavas,
105	3	sentiment,	sentiment.
132	16	प्रचश्नते	प्रचक्षते
142	8	प्रकरी	प्रकारी
144	15	juster	jester
146	4	seperated	separated
,,	9	characteirsties.	characteristics
,,	24	nability	inability.
155	3	jewellry	jewellery.
159	18	yet	yet,
164	25	are	is
178	1	innermist	innermost
,,	12	to	refers to